More Praise for

MARKETING FOR TOMORROW, NOT YESTERDAY

"CMOs today face unprecedented challenges. They need to quickly determine the best way to connect with audiences and engage in a rapidly changing environment. The channels of insight—digital, social, multi-channel, and more—must be continually mastered. At the same time, the demands of a range of constituents, from sales associates to shareholders to the CEO, have to be met or exceeded. Fortunately, Zain Raj helps sort out what is important, what is essential, and what isn't worth the time. Zain not only has the experience to bring his theory to life, he also shares it in a relatable and pragmatic way that makes it easy to put into practice. It strikes just the right balance between the conceptual and the practical."

—Gary E. Hendrickson, Chairman and CEO, The Valspar Corporation

"The complexity of today's business landscape continues to challenge marketers. Zain has once again provided practical, rational insights that every marketer can benefit from. If you're wondering how to become a 'tomorrow decathlete' read this book."

—Michael Grasso, Chief Marketing Officer, Sunrun

"Marketing in today's world means you have to be ready to change and evolve quickly. You have to keep up. Zain's book, *Marketing for Tomorrow*, shows you just how to navigate the rough waters, to find the answers to help your business thrive, and to not get left behind in the dust."

—Cecilia K. McKenney, Executive Vice President and Chief Customer Officer, Frontier Communications

MARKETING FOR TOMORROW, NOT YESTERDAY

MARKETING FOR TOMORROW, NOT YESTERDAY

Surviving and Thriving
in the Insight Economy™

ZAIN RAJ

Spyglass Publishing, LLC
Chicago, IL

For more information contact:
Spyglass Publishing, LLC
153 W. Ohio St., STE 300
Chicago, IL 60654
312-321-8104

Hardcover: 978-0-9967268-0-1
eBook: 978-0-9967268-1

Library of Congress Control Number: 2015913591

To my parents,
who taught me to dream...
May you both look down on us
and like what you see.

CONTENTS

CHAPTER 1 Everything's Changed, But Not
Everyone's Paying Attention 1

CHAPTER 2 Why CMOs Struggle to Keep Up 11

CHAPTER 3 You've Got to Be a *Marketing Decathlete*™, 25
Not a One-Sport Wonder

CHAPTER 4 Where Social, Big Data, IoT, Mobile, 51
and Micro-Segmentation Really Lead

CHAPTER 5 From the Attention Economy to Attention 69
Deficit Disorder: How Even Great
Companies Got Lost in the Transition
to the Insight Economy

CHAPTER 6 Embracing the Insight Economy 81

CHAPTER 7 Who You Are When You Aren't Trying 97
to Be Someone Else?

CHAPTER 8 Stop Marketing to People Who Aren't 113
Your Customers (and Who Never Will Be)

CHAPTER 9   Living the Promise: What Brands Must   127
Stand for Today

CHAPTER 10   Give Consumers *Real* Reasons to Buy   141
Your Products

CHAPTER 11   The Real Question: Are You Thinking   157
About the Future of Your Business?

Continued About the Author Bio   *163*

Chapter 1

Everything's Changed, But Not Everyone's Paying Attention

HAVE YOU EVER been somewhere—a meeting, a party, an event, a family dinner—where everyone seems to be talking to you all at once? It's impossible to sort out, even for the best listener. There are important stories, juicy gossip, action items, and anecdotes to process, but you can't make out any single thing over the din. Instead of sparkling conversation, you're drowning in a torrent of sound.

Today's Chief Marketing Officers (CMOs) face this kind of dilemma—one that drives even the best of them nuts. It doesn't matter if they've been in the industry for decades, pioneered best practices, and built the gold standards; they're now living in an exciting—albeit terrifying—time in both the marketing ecosystem and the world at large. Jeff Hayzlett, the former CMO of Kodak, said it best when he exclaimed, "This shit is scary!"

No matter how much we think we know about marketing in today's fascinating, frenetic climate, there's always more to learn. Even the most seasoned among us are in danger of finding ourselves blinded to those lessons by old habits or lack of information.

For the last thirty years, I've been immersed in the same changing tides you have. I've kept from sinking, fashioning myself into a pretty good swimmer along the way, and I'm happy to share what I've learned with you in the hope that we can make it out of the cacophony around us and find some clarity together.

        • • •

Like all good stories, mine involves a bit of a journey. It begins in India in the 1980s, when I was at the University of Bombay majoring in economics and finance. I had just passed the exam to become a CPA, and I thought my path was set. I was ready to put my blinders on. But when I attended an elective seminar as part of a new program the university was offering on advertising, I felt as if I'd been struck by lightning. This was the path for me. Advertising took what I had been learning about the mechanics of business and connected it with creativity by putting it in a framework of big ideas.

In 1984, the advertising industry in the United States was heralding a shift from the Attention Economy (think big brands, the time of the Don Drapers and the real Mad Men) to the Information Economy, led by data-driven companies like Amazon and Google. In India, the practice of marketing and advertising were just getting started. At the time when my business life was just beginning, my country was reeling from shock; the day before my first day on the job at my first ad agency, Prime Minister Indira Gandhi had been assassinated. The streets were totally empty as I walked to work. But when I got to the office, I wasn't alone; the owner of the firm,

Mrs. Nargis Wadia, and the head of client services, Farid Karim, had come in, too. Despite my subordinate role—bringing them tea—I was able to sit in on some high-level strategy meetings, absorbing all I could from day one.

Over the years, I've worked in large and small firms in India and the United States. After beginning my career at Interpublicity, I went to the India division of Grey Advertising, where I learned the intricacies of integrated marketing across a number of different categories. Since coming to the United States in 1990, I've led global client assignments at agencies like J. Walter Thompson; Foote, Cone & Belding; and Havas Worldwide while building successful and future-oriented global marketing services capabilities for these and other large advertising agencies—FCBi for Interpublic and Euro RSCG Discovery for Havas. I also built a couple of entrepreneurial companies over the years. BrandXP was one of the earliest digitally led strategy firms, which I created in the early 2000s. Most recently, I built Hyper Marketing, the largest independent marketing services company in North America before we sold it to Alliance Data Systems in 2012.

Despite these different experiences, I'm still as excited and still as passionate as I was that first day over thirty years ago. But while my passion for marketing hasn't changed, the landscape of the business certainly has. There's been the shift from the Attention Economy (1960–1984) to the Information Economy (1985–2014), but now we're in the middle of another shift, which we'll talk more about later in the book: a shift to an era that I have dubbed the *Insight Economy*™. The Insight Economy requires us to translate and transform the huge amount of information that has become available, in order to find new avenues for growth by leveraging powerful and compelling insights that help us serve our customers' real needs. If you haven't been able to pay close attention, you may not have noticed the subtle changes in all aspects of business and marketing. The majority of these changes are seismic, and they're picking up speed.

PEOPLE AND PROCESS

First and foremost, the very fabric of the marketing ecosystem has changed over time. Here, I'm speaking of the *people* who comprise that fabric, both the marketers and the consumers. When I began in the business, marketers were highly specialized professionals working at companies, directing their marketing and advertising investments. On the other hand, these marketers also worked for agencies that specialized in brand advertising, direct marketing, sales promotions, or public relations. The marketing support industry was very fragmented, each piece resting comfortably in its silo. You wouldn't find a particularly holistic approach anywhere; you'd go to the specialist you needed for each piece of the puzzle. The pace of things was predictably slow—it would take a year or two to launch a big product with a big commercial splash (like Apple's "1984" launch ad that aired during the Super Bowl).

The data coming back from these campaigns would trickle in slowly, too. In India, we launched campaigns for new products on Sunday nights—the one night that you could count on people watching television, because that was the only night that Doordarshan, the

Indian government's channel, would screen popular movies. We'd have our research people standing in retail stores during the commercial break (we had just one break in the middle of the movie, during which all commercials were aired, one after the other) to see if the ad campaign was working—if we saw people running in to buy the new product, we'd know it was successful. This was our way to get real-time results. You may be a bit skeptical about this story, but it is true.

Even in the 1990s, the data we used to measure a campaign's impact took us as long as three months to obtain. I'm sure you remember Nielsen and IRI sales and share reports. We would get them monthly, but it would take us at least three months to get a handle on how the product or service was performing in the market. Remember BASES? It took us six to nine months to get results from one test. Test markets used to run for months, and an advertising campaign took years to develop and execute.

But now we've entered a whole new era. When a commercial airs, we see instantaneous response and reaction via social channels and digital analytics. As this timeline has compressed, the world of marketing has become far less linear and far less disciplined than it was during the time of the specialists and the slow-cooked messages. It is now a far more chaotic, nonlinear set of activities that sometimes feels incoherent. There's not time to focus on one area or one metric anymore; we've got to be everywhere at once, and we have to be there now.

The change in people and process extends to the structure of the businesses themselves. If you look at the companies making up the Dow, they comprise a very different picture today than they did thirty years ago. Those classic staples and blue-chip companies that stood on top thirty years ago (most of which were led by older white men with Ivy League pedigrees) have given way to disruptive startups run by innovative thirty-somethings. Companies like Woolworth, Bethlehem Steel, and American Can are no longer around. Google, Facebook, Apple, Amazon, Uber—these companies don't offer commodities in the traditional sense, and yet their high-flying valuations should give pause to the consumer-products giants of yore.

GOING GLOBAL

Shortly after I moved to the United States in the summer of 1991, I interviewed with a couple of senior executives at a well-known, worldwide advertising firm. One of them asked me how we got around in India. "Do you guys still ride on camels and elephants?" he asked. I summoned as much equanimity as I could and informed him that we saved the camels and elephants for special occasions but got around in automobiles. I was being a smart aleck, but I couldn't let that ignorant comment pass unanswered.

Needless to say, I didn't get the job. But looking back at that time, the incident strikes me as both unsurprising and shocking. It was unsurprising because even in the early '90s, in the melting pot of the United States, I found myself in a very structured and parochial society; it was shocking because even though the advertising agency in question had been founded by a Scot and had international reach and global clientele, its leadership in Chicago didn't know how to deal with a brown face that showed up looking for a job. Even though we were essentially functioning as a global economy (in a global industry), we hadn't been sensitized to being global.

That parochial country has now become a leader in the larger, global village defined by Marshall McLuhan in 1964 (the year after my birth). We recognize our ties more readily; we recognize that when a tiny country such as Cyprus sneezes, we in the U.S. end up catching a cold—as the U.S. stock markets did when the Cyprus stock market collapsed in March 2013. Trends in one country directly affect another, for worse and for better. We've also become more aware of the environment, the fragile fabric that stretches above and beneath all of us; doing good, being good, and being healthy are all platform trends in the global market.

COMMUNICATION: FROM CONTROL TO CHAOS

When I first started in the business world, we communicated by Telex (yes, *Telex*). We carried huge, handwritten whiteboards to meetings to give presentations. We had one assistant to take dictation for all correspondence, and another to take messages and serve coffee or tea. The biggest innovation of the time was overhead projectors, which we'd lug into meetings instead of the aforementioned whiteboards; this was great, because now we were able to use a few different transparencies instead of having to erase and scribble over smudges from an earlier presentation. Telephones were scarce; there were no mobile phones, but only the regular, corded landline phones. This created a number of communication challenges. I remember not being able to call home when my flight from Calcutta to New Delhi was canceled, and, arriving home a day later, finding my wife understandably upset.

It sounds quaint at best, and like a bad joke at worst. I couldn't even begin to explain this to many of the people I work with today, much less my kids, who have grown up in an era in which everyone has a tiny mobile computer in his or her pocket at all times—and I mean *at all times*. We've gone from a society that used to communicate in a controlled, analog manner to one that lives in a constant cacophony of content. We create, consume, and critique faster than ever before. We no longer need time to comparison shop or drive from one end of town to the other. We can pay bills from a plane thousands of feet in the air, eschew the mall in favor of Cyber Monday, and streamline our commerce and communication in one fell swoop.

The flip side of this explosion of content is a paucity of available attention with which to sort it out. Now, as we enter the Insight Economy, we find ourselves dealing with the fundamental issue of *time starvation*—a problem that we've brought on ourselves. The assault of content, the creation and consumption, means that we live in an always-on and always-distracted world. Consumers are constantly encouraged to engage, interact with, and digest this content, thereby enabling marketers to obtain more data. In order to make decisions in this era of time starvation, we've had to rely on shortcuts such as sound bites—and this is true for both consumers and those who drive consumer strategy. We're surrounded by static and noise of our own making, and the only way we can hope to get out ahead of the game, rather than remaining stuck in the past, is to devise a prism through which we can focus our point of view in order to make some sense of this madness and truly pay attention to the important things in the world around us.

COMMITTING TO CHANGE

So what gives? If we're all so smart and better informed than ever, if we're all armed with more data, more insights, and more content than ever, why are so many of us failing to truly pay attention and change the way we approach marketing in the Insight Economy?

Part of the reason is, no doubt, confusion resulting from the time starvation we talked about before. Part of it is that it's quite impossible to pay attention to everything all at once, so we stick to what we know. Particularly in the business world, legacy companies get so wrapped up in their own histories (and in the approaches that have netted them so much wealth in the past) that they find it hard to see other ways to operate. The more overwhelmed CMOs get, the more they are asked to do, and the more that they're used as ceremonial whipping boys when things don't go right, the more often we see strategic focus slip through the cracks of tactical execution.

I would love to present a simple solution for you, but I'm afraid to say that nothing about this process is going to be simple. The solution to any complex problem has to be complex—but that doesn't mean it has to be complicated. And it certainly doesn't mean it has to be dry, impossible, or without the rewards that come from harnessing the transformative power of change. Today's marketing industry needs its star performers to be decathletes, achieving strength in multiple disciplines in a chaotic, multidimensional economy. More than ever before, CMOs are being held accountable. Their remit is very clear. Their CEOs and boards are asking for distinctive and compelling *ideas* that will deliver strong results—measurable business outcomes that they can take to the street. Finding big, new ideas and new ways to differentiate brands has become today's biggest unsolved business problem.

CMOs are on the line when ideas fail, and when that happens, they find themselves out on the streets as more and more boards and CEOs decide that traditional marketing capability is a replaceable skill. To avoid this fate, you, as a marketing leader today, need to make yourself irreplaceable. You need to hone your focus, broaden your skill set, and learn how to formulate powerful ideas that can transform your brand and the business.

As we move further through this book, I will lay out proven principles and actions that will help you play to win. This will enable us to change the perception of marketers as (M)ad Men who merely affect consumer beliefs to an image of marketers as business leaders who transform customer behavior. And we will do this in a way that allows you to smile all the way to the bank.

CHAPTER 2

Why CMOs Struggle to Keep Up

THERE WAS A TIME when the CMO's seat was a cushy one. Once reserved for the crème de la crème, the time-tested veteran who had put in the long hours and grueling ladder-climbing we expect of our executives, the CMO's throne was the best seat in the house.

Now it's just the hot seat.

If you're in this position, you know what I'm talking about. You know how it feels to be inundated with questions from your board and your CEO. Or how it can seem that no matter how long and hard you work, you're never going to be able to keep up with all the information, all the trends, and all the technology that you've got coming at you 24/7. Innovation seems like something to be feared, rather than embraced. It can feel like you're no longer able to see the forest for the trees. It can feel, in fact, as if you're absolutely lost in that forest—and in truth, you probably are.

The role of the CMO has been evolving for quite some time. When I started out thirty years ago—and even well before I came on the scene—CMOs were specialists with concentrated expertise in a single area. With only one ball to keep their eyes on, they were able to take their time and produce carefully constructed results (and products, and brands, and so on). That's no longer the case. To keep up with the hectic pace of today's consumers (and the competition), CMOs have to step up their game radically if they hope to remain relevant and successful.

We are on a swift trajectory of change, one that shows no sign of slowing down. So you can forget about transforming your environment. The only hope for you, beleaguered, bewildered CMO, is to stop being a one-sport wonder and turn yourself into a *Marketing Decathlete*™.

THE WAY WE WERE:
THE ROLE OF CMOS IN PREHISTORIC TIMES

Back in the day, CMOs and other senior marketers fell into two categories: brand marketers and response marketers. **Brand marketers** were charged with creating, positioning, and promoting what were called the "big ideas"—the association of a particular product with an emotional driver or the connection of a "lifestyle" to that brand, for instance. Marketing was where it was at, and the big brands themselves were the ones advancing the field, institutionalizing strategy and tactics. If you were a thought leader in marketing during this era, you were probably working for one of the consumer packaged-goods companies like Procter & Gamble, Colgate, or Unilever, constructing marketing strategy and positioning frameworks that would change the game for your brands and that would become common practice for others in the field. Brand marketers ruled the roost.

Response marketers were the other type of "experts" common in this era. Unlike the brand marketers, these guys were hyper-focused on delivering measurable results by using direct marketing and data-driven programs. These were folks in financial institutions, insurance companies, and so on. They were all about customer acquisition, and they knew how to use the data they collected to drive offers and target their marketing to achieve that end. There was, obviously, some tension between the response marketers—who were focused on delivering transactions—and the brand marketers, who contended that the brand itself was the MVP who fostered the public's good will and brought value to the business.

Both types of marketers were largely part of a generation of people now in their forties and fifties—men and women who grew up in an ecosystem that was much more specialized and slower-paced than the world of marketing today (or the world, period). And when I say "slower-paced," I mean slower about everything from the bottom up. Time seemed to expand for the workforce itself; a brand marketer at Procter & Gamble could expect to internalize P&G's approach and systems, in part because he was likely to be at the company for decades. Lifetime employment seemed a given; CMOs had what amounted to tenure in their companies and could speak to institutional change and developments with authority.

By contrast, nowadays the workforce is flooded with remote-working, flextime-taking, sure-footed, quicksilvery millennials who will see not one or two, but eight or nine employers (or even careers) in their lifetimes. In the past, being laid off was an unsightly black mark on one's resumé, but it's now a matter of course. I recently had dinner with an old colleague who spoke of the likelihood of his impending layoff with something resembling excitement. He was already making plans for what he would do in the downtime between this job and the next one, and reimagining his career in a different industry.

SO WHAT'S CHANGED? CHANGE ITSELF, FOR ONE THING!

The world was different then. Back then, you could count on being around long enough to see several small changes occur, such as packaging tweaks (a new, more conveniently shaped toothpaste cap) or resizing ("Now with 10% more XYZ!") to attract attention on the shelves. The change that these CMOs were used to for decades was incremental, but now we talk about change that is exponential. This change snowballs, strengthening itself as it goes. It's not just products that are transforming, but entire *categories*. For example, Wrigley (which, not coincidentally, has gone through four CMOs in the last five years) used to have to compete in a fairly stable category: gum and confection. The name Wrigley was synonymous with gum, and vice versa. But now it's competing not only with other brands of gum, but also with items such as yogurt, mints, and breath-freshening sprays and strips.

Not only do CMOs today face rapidly changing categories, but the competition within those categories has exploded, thanks largely to the Internet. In the old days, the CMO of a company like PetSmart would face relatively clear-cut competition: He'd be vying for customers with the likes of Petco, Petland, and independent pet retailers. Now there are dozens of brands online that deliver directly to consumers, not to mention the eight-hundred-pound gorilla in every room—Amazon. Even optometrists and quick-service brick-and-mortar operations like Pearle Vision and LensCrafters have to compete with e-tailers like Warby Parker, where bespectacled buyers can try on glasses in the comfort of their living rooms and use free shipping for a quick turnaround at a fraction of the cost. My brother-in-law recently used Eye Buy Direct to get not just one replacement for his older glasses, but *three* new frames for the price of his old one that he'd gotten from his local optometrist. What's not to like? I definitely sympathize with the consumer who feels like convenience is a deal breaker (or a deal maker). And thanks to today's technology and new business models, that doesn't mean having to compromise on quality, customer service, or customization. It's really a win-win for the consumer, and for companies that deliver new services in new ways.

The very nature of consumption is changing to mirror these shifts in category and competition. Consumers today are primed to click their mice before they click their seatbelts, and big-box stores are consolidating and even closing their doors (Circuit City, Radio Shack, Montgomery Ward, anyone?) in the face of a shopping experience that offers more comfort and convenience than brick-and-mortar shopping centers can provide. The role of the consumer has changed, too: The consumer is becoming the curator of his or her own experience rather than a passive recipient (and thanks to social media, providing real-time *Consumer Reports*-like reviews for his or her own audience).

We see this in the retail industry with "hauling," the perfect marriage of the millennial generation's two favorite things: Technology and shopping. *Hauler* is a term for a tech-savvy young fashionista who shows off her purchases (or "hauls") in a homemade video that she posts online. There are now more than 700,000 haul videos on YouTube, and they form one of the fastest-growing categories. A successful video can garner hundreds of thousands of views and turn a hauler into a beauty guru with a huge fan base. Hauling is effective in influencing teens' buying choices because the hauler is seen as authentic and relatable. Because of this, the FTC has ruled that haulers must disclose to their viewers which products they have been given for free. Retailers including Target, JC Penney, Urban Outfitters, Forever 21, and others are participating in hauling in some form or other.

Likewise, the roles of marketers in corporations are no longer clearly defined. Where there were once people who specialized in research and insights, advertising, direct marketing, brand management, and so on, now marketing teams are smaller and expected to react more quickly than ever with new ideas and new products. The timelines have sped up. I remember working with Motorola, helping them transition from the brick phone to the MicroTAC (the first real consumer cell phone) and then the StarTAC, which was the company's and the world's first flip phone (imagine: a *flip phone* as an advance in technology!) and doing all of this with three- and five-year plans mapped out for product launches and advertising campaigns. Like the flip phone, however, long-term strategic plans are a thing of the past—change happens far too swiftly now for anyone to plan farther ahead than the next year.

This compression of time and blurring of capabilities means that there are no longer "experts," and there are no longer "gold standard" or "best practice" channels and tools with which these experts must work. Gone are the days when someone could specialize in marketing or branding and perfect an approach over time. Gone are the rigor and quality control for publication of content by thought leaders; instead, you're one voice among hundreds, or thousands! Self-publishing and the proliferation of the Internet and social media channels have taken the shine off the designation of *expert*, if not eliminated it entirely. Now anyone with an opinion and time on his hands can be followed, linked, and favorited into the status of "expert." There is no dearth of experts with new buzzwords and methods, all claiming to help marketers make sense out of all this information. Here are some interesting data points (found on Google, July 10, 2014):

- 51 million search results for the term *Insight Experts*
- 143 million search results for the term *Big Data Experts*
- 7.48 million search results for the term *Analytic Experts*

I claim to be one of these experts. Despite being the author of a bestseller in sales and marketing, I don't even show up in the Google search results for *Insight Experts* until page 113. This is a bit embarrassing, but illuminating.

And finally, as I've hinted with all this talk about the Internet and social media, there's been a change in the way we create, absorb, and respond to content, both as marketers and as consumers. For the consumer, this content explosion means that consumers are more overwhelmed than ever before by marketing information—they're being reached in real time on multiple platforms by all kinds of promotional and transactional messages. For CMOs, this means having to craft channel-specific content (and monitor channel-specific insights) for a slew of channels that didn't exist when many of you started out in the business. Where we used to have to worry about positioning for TV, print, radio, and outdoor campaigns—at fairly predictable prices—we now have to tangle with all of the above *plus* on-demand television *plus* streaming video *plus* digital radio *plus* Netflix *plus* YouTube *plus* Facebook *plus* Twitter *plus, plus, plus*. And there's fragmentation within each of these channels, too. There's simply not enough time, resources, or bandwidth to keep up with all the complexity a CMO has to deal with today.

TECHNOLOGY, TOYS, AND TACTICS: THE CHICKEN OR THE EGG OF CHANGE

The good old days of being a CMO were truly great if you were looking for lifetime employment, a steady career trajectory, and a predictable workday. They were particularly great for veterans of the industry, if for no other reason than the fact that when you're older, you're less able to adapt and learn—the neural pathways have been built and strengthened over time and the neurons in your brain fire more slowly than those of your younger colleagues.

A very dear friend who was a long-tenured CMO for a top-ten retail organization retired last year. "I just got tired of running hard all the time only to find myself still standing in the same spot," she said. She was exhausted by the constant pressure to get, process, and then act on all the data coming in 24/7. "It was hard to respond strategically to any of it ... I didn't enjoy being tactically minded in all my marketspace responses."

While I understand why all this change and the resultant complexity seem intimidating, I don't think it has to be seen in a negative light. I think it can be a truly great thing, an opportunity for the creative and the willing among us to embrace the new tide. The rewards are undeniable. I'm personally of the mind that living in a period of such monumental change is unbelievably exciting, like being a creature in the Cambrian Period, when evolution really began to ratchet up.

For the science and geology geeks among us, the Cambrian Period marked a profound change in life on Earth. Prior to this time, the majority of living organisms were small, simple, unicellular organisms. Complex, multicellular organisms had gradually become more common over the millions of years immediately preceding the Cambrian, but it was not until this period that mineralized— and hence readily fossilized—organisms became common. The rapid diversification of life-forms in the Cambrian Period, known as the Cambrian explosion, produced the first representatives of all modern animal phyla. That's very similar to the changes in the digital, social, and mobile ecosystems we've seen over the past decade and ones that'll continue into the next few.

On the other hand, for folks like me who are into arts and culture, it is like being a disciple of one of the Renaissance masters, like Michelangelo, Leonardo da Vinci or Raphael. I revel in innovation and consider myself fortunate enough to have started my career on the cusp of this great change thirty years ago, as opposed to cutting my teeth during the "golden age" of advertising, the period of *Mad Men* that preceded my entrance into the industry. I understand and empathize with the fact that dealing with such rapid change is an uphill battle for many of our colleagues in the marketing world, with an incredibly steep learning curve.

Much of this learning curve has to do with the technology available today. Change is enabled and accelerated by technology, and vice versa; it's a chicken-or-the-egg scenario whose circular pattern is accelerated by a younger, more flexible workforce taking over for the boomer generation as it phases into retirement. These new workers are able to adapt more swiftly to change, but they're also the ones largely driving that change. And I'm experiencing it firsthand.

My son recently became the head of marketing for the business fraternity Alpha Kappa Psi at the Kelley School of Business at Indiana University. He responded to an announcement from the fraternity that it was looking for candidates interested in this position. In my old days, for an opportunity like this, I would simply submit a resumé and a cover letter, carefully written and spell-checked to ensure a good impression and an invitation to an interview. However Aamir decided to approach this opportunity in a way that surprised me but which was completely natural to him. He used his grasp of digital technologies to make his application stand out from those of the other respondents, even though they were his peers. How did he do this? Instead of delivering his resumé as a Word or PDF document, he created a video commercial that brought his passion and his qualifications to life. He posted the video on his YouTube channel and submitted a digital version of his résumé with a link to the video to the committee responsible for screening and hiring the right candidate. Guess what? He got the job and he got it right away, and he's having a blast in his role expanding AKPsi's membership among the business students at Indiana University. He was able to use his creativity and the tools available to him to make something wonderful on the fly. Technology is the enabler of this moment in our industry's evolution, and it is available to all of us to use in different and creative ways to meet our business and marketing objectives.

All this technology—particularly in the social and mobile spheres—has made real-time responses to content a necessary investment for every organization. Consumers are responding to *your* content in real time, and they expect you to respond to *their* content in real time, too. CMOs are just as responsible for PR and reputation management as they are for driving sales and delivering data on campaigns.

On January 8, 2015, *Ad Age* published a story about a study conducted by the Gartner research firm in collaboration with the CMO Club, which revealed that CMOs say top management is increasingly expecting them to lead their organizations' *entire customer experience*. At the same time, they admit their progress in doing so is lacking.

Customer experience is the practice of centralizing customer data in an effort to provide customers with the best possible interactions with every part of the company, from marketing to sales and even finance. The Gartner study found that 25 percent of CMOs say leading customer experience is the most-increased expectation

CEOs have of them over the last year. It beat out the next category, developing and retaining staff, by 11 percentage points.

But Gartner also asked marketers about the areas in which they've made the most progress—and customer experience came in last. "It's a new expectation and it's a difficult expectation," said Laura McLellan, VP of marketing strategies at Gartner and author of the report. Ms. McLellan said the opportunity to lead customer-experience efforts is an opportunity for CMOs to gain more influence within their companies, but they risk leaving that influence on the table if they don't take the reins soon.

Imagine that! Not just creating advertising campaigns to bring customers in, or building a brand that customers desire and respond to, but everything from innovations to operations to damage control. Sometimes those final two go hand in hand; look at what happened when Tropicana dared to change its classic packaging … and had to backpedal when the social media backlash began.

Tropicana introduced new packaging on January 8, 2009, scrapping the twenty-four-year-old design that had made the brand an icon. Tropicana had sought to create excitement around the Pure Premium rebrand, announcing a "historic integrated marketing and advertising campaign … designed to reinforce the brand and product attributes, rejuvenate the category, and help consumers rediscover the health benefits they get from drinking America's iconic orange juice brand." It discontinued the longtime Tropicana brand symbol, an orange with a protruding straw. The symbol, meant to evoke fresh taste, was supplanted on the new packages by a glass of orange juice.

Immediately, consumers began to complain about the makeover in letters, e-mails, and telephone calls. Some of the consumer comments described the new packaging as "ugly" or "stupid," and resembling "a generic bargain brand" or a "store brand." "Do any of these package-design people actually shop for orange juice?" the writer of one e-mail message asked rhetorically. "Because I do, and the new cartons stink." Others complained that the redesign made it more difficult to distinguish among the varieties of Tropicana or to differentiate Tropicana from other orange juices. On the business front, after its package redesign, sales of the Tropicana Pure Premium line plummeted 20 percent between January 1 and February 22, costing the brand tens of millions of dollars.

The PepsiCo Americas Beverages division of PepsiCo bowed to public demand and scrapped the changes it had made to its flagship product, Tropicana Pure Premium orange juice. The redesigned packaging was discontinued and the previous version was brought back within a month.

The normal response of the outnumbered CMO is to be overcome by channel confusion, content explosion, and the data deluge that comes in 24/7 from every source and every angle. Is it any wonder that many CMOs are unable to unearth actionable insights from this mountain of material? Is it surprising that the average CMO feels overwhelmed by the data pouring in, unable to respond adequately to each individual observation or opportunity to put together a cohesive strategy?

I don't think so, but I'm a very sympathetic audience. While I'm one of those rare and geeky birds who hasn't succumbed to the technology terror yet—I rather like change—I understand that for most, it's a lot to deal with. But I also understand that not every innovation or cool new app is going to necessitate a rewrite of the playbook. Most of the innovations we talk about in meetings or that are presented at exciting conferences like the annual Consumer Electronics Show (CES) shouldn't be seen as silver bullets. Nanotechnology and artificial intelligence aren't going to become the industry standard for marketers (or any other industry) anytime soon. But it's my view that we should see all of this change and potential as something to embrace—without going down rabbit holes of terrifying possibilities that may very well come to nothing (Google Glass, anyone?).

So what's an overwhelmed, overworked CMO to do? I advocate pulling back from specialties and specifics, because there's no way you're going to accomplish all that you need to by being one of those one-sport wonders. You need to become, as I've said, a Marketing Decathlete. You need to reframe the situation so that all of this change is to your advantage. You need to look at available technology as a strategic asset rather than simply as a tactical tool. You need to understand that there is no time to be hyper-focused on one specific area of expertise, but instead use your strategic acumen and your ability not only to affect consumers' attitudes and beliefs, but also to affect their behaviors.

It's hard to see the forest for the trees when you're so busy running, ducking, zigging, and zagging that you can't see how to cut a clear path. Instead of getting lost in those trees, start focusing on the forest. Trust me, the view is better.

CHAPTER 3

You've Got to Be a *Marketing Decathlete*™, Not a One-Sport Wonder

DALEY THOMPSON

The next time you find yourself in the presence of one of those insufferable people who know way too much about far too many trivial sporting events and figures, politely ask if they know who the world's greatest athlete might be. That's the title given to the winner of the men's decathlon in the Olympic Games, a tradition that started with the great Jim Thorpe in 1912.

When I was growing up in India, the one event I watched from beginning to end (other than cricket of course) was the Olympics. It would be telecast at odd hours, depending on which country was hosting. And the one event I never missed was the Decathlon. During that period, the world's greatest athlete was a decathlete from the U.K.—perhaps the greatest athlete ever produced by the British Empire. Often compared to the legendary Jesse Owens, Daley Thompson dominated the decathlon for nearly a decade. Between 1978 and 1986, he won two Olympic gold medals, three gold medals in the Commonwealth Games (once known as the British Empire

Games), and two more in the European Championships. In 1983, when he won the gold medal at the World Championships in Helsinki, Finland, he held every major decathlon title on the planet. No one since has come close to equaling Thompson's world-beating prowess.

That said, he was anything but a lovable guy. Fiercely competitive, caustic, profane, unpredictable, unmanageable, he certainly would not have been an attractive brand spokesperson in today's politically correct world. Nevertheless, I'm not at all hesitant to recommend him as a role model for savvy marketers who wish to remain relevant—and employable—in the economy of the future.

To put it simply, I believe the decathlon is an increasingly apt metaphor for the varied forms of intense competition that define marketing today. And whether you choose Jesse Owens, Daley Thompson, or Ashton Eaton (the American who took the gold at the 2012 Olympics in London) as your competitive icon—or America's Jackie Joyner-Kersee (named the greatest female athlete of the twentieth century by *Sports Illustrated*), Great Britain's Jessica Ennis (the 2012 Olympic gold medalist in the women's heptathlon), or Ukraine's Hanna Melnychenko (winner of the 2013 World Championship in Athletics)—it's their sustained excellence at facing a spectrum of challenges that makes them noteworthy for the purpose of our discussion.

It may seem a bit counterintuitive to say that it's not good enough to be a one-sport wonder. After all, isn't Usain Bolt a huge star? Or Michael Johnson? There seems to be nothing wrong with being at the top of your field in one sport or event. In the old days of the business world, when CMOs and the like were one-sport star performers as either brand or response marketers, it worked. But given the complexity and incoherence in the environment now, the real stars today are the Marketing Decathletes—the guys and gals who are proficient at different events in a sustainable way. The ones who have the alacrity and the endurance to get to the finish line even after tackling numerous challenges. They don't have to be the *best* at any *one* activity; what makes them decathletes is their ability to be *good* at the *ten* marketing areas. The Greeks devised the decathlon as an overall holistic test of an athlete's prowess in every sense. The new business environment challenges marketers today to do the same.

My intent here is not to make you an instant expert on international track and field competition. Rather, it's to provide a little context to explain why I believe this form of competition corresponds to what marketers are facing today and will face in the years to come. In contrast to years past, when specialization was the order of the day, today's real test of marketing expertise is an ability to compete in a variety of ways, and to succeed not by excelling at any one thing, but by being able to at least hold our own—and in some cases excel—at many.

Back to Daley Thompson. Thompson was a decorated Olympic decathlete, a man who won two gold medals in the event and broke the world record for that series of ten challenges four times. He was considered the best athlete in the world, not because he could break land speed records in the hundred-meter dash like Usain Bolt, or hurdle like Michael Johnson. While he could hold his own if you were to pit him against either of these amazing athletes, it's unlikely that he could take them down. But if you were to put either of these guys up against him in a decathlon? They wouldn't have a chance. While they trained for specific situations, Thompson trained for everything. While they could push their muscles to the breaking point for the precise amount of time needed to complete a hundred-meter run or four-hundred-meter hurdle event, Thompson's entire muscular system was primed to be able to jump, run, *and* throw in ten events over the course of two days. The decathlon tests an athlete's ability to survive and adapt in a brutal, changing world.

This is a metaphor, of course—I don't expect to see Apple CEO Tim Cook throwing a javelin for his paycheck any time soon—but it's an apt one. To be able to survive in the hyper-complex, multifaceted Insight Economy, we have to look at the decathlete marketers: the men and women who have successfully mastered ten trades instead of focusing on only one, to the detriment of the big picture.

STEPPING UP TO THE PODIUM ...

I want to start by introducing you to four specific Marketing Decathletes. They are by no means the only success stories in our field, but they are clear examples of what it means to be a Marketing Decathlete. Their backgrounds are as diverse as their current roles and assignments, but they all had the big-picture acumen needed to evolve beyond their original specialties. In the last chapter, we talked about how unlikely it is these days that you'll live and breathe the same company—or even the same industry—for your entire career before retiring with a nice pension and a gold-plated watch. These executives have shown that no matter the market segment, no matter the product or service, and no matter the battering their businesses have taken from the forces of change, they're able to survive and thrive because they've honed a broad set of skills rather than just having focused on one specific area of expertise.

Tom O'Toole is our first decathlete. Tom is chief marketing officer for United Airlines and president of Mileage Plus Holdings, the United Continental Holdings loyalty program. He is now well established in the big-ticket, high-pressure airline industry, and he has a gold-plated reputation as one of the best loyalty marketers in the world. But that's a far cry from where he started. Tom grew up in the world of technology and IT, rising through the ranks at Hyatt to oversee technology worldwide for the hotel chain. After rising from CTO to become head of global marketing there, he was able to parlay his skills into a much bigger and much more challenging role in a new arena, where he has used his abilities to redefine the concept of loyalty.

Cecilia McKenney came up in the HR world, first at Pepsi Bottling Group and now at Frontier Communications Corp, a major player in the Telco world, where she's Executive Vice President & Chief Customer Officer. When Frontier reorganized its Senior Leadership Team, Maggie Wilderotter, the CEO, asked Cecilia to take over responsibility for marketing at a time that was critical for the evolution of the Frontier business and reputation. A natural decathlete, she rose to the challenge and inspired her marketing team, her company, and her agencies, to develop a marketing campaign based on powerful insights and inspired ideas. (You should check out Frank, the Frontier buffalo, at frontier.com/frankscorner.) Within six months, this approach and program enabled Frontier to outperform its competitors, including big companies like Comcast and Time Warner. According to Morgan Stanley, "Frank the Buffalo helped Frontier outperform all others," leading to its announced acquisition of Verizon assets in California, Florida, and Texas, doubling the size of its business.

Michael Grasso, now CMO for SunRun, a solar energy firm, cut his teeth in the world of data and technology, where he worked for the likes of AT&T and USAA before moving on to become CMO of TXU Energy. The energy market in Texas, where TXU is based, recently had been deregulated, and more than fifty competitors were now fighting for their share of eight million households—and competing on price. Michael knew how to strategically leverage a powerful insight into his customers that all of these fifty-plus competitors missed: That they wanted their energy provider to help them spend less on their energy, not just promise cheap energy for a short promotional period. He used this insight to develop a compelling idea that leveraged big data and deep technology capabilities to deliver a digitally led solution that reshaped the commoditized energy marketplace and put TXU in a strong growth position. Michael Grasso had a number of the skills and capabilities required of a Marketing Decathlete, as we'll discuss later on in the chapter.

Finally, I'd like you to meet **John Costello,** a wonderful example of a classic yet contemporary marketer who has successfully transitioned from a traditional CPG marketing background. Costello reinvented Sears with a brilliant strategic ploy, playing up "the softer side of Sears." He went on to lead a start-up and helped reinvent one of today's most mainstream brands.

He started at Procter & Gamble—the Harvard of brand marketing, as we've noted earlier. There's no doubt that Procter & Gamble is successful at what it does, but in today's Insight Economy, much more is demanded and needed of CMOs. John gets this better than most, and brings this level of strategic clarity with customer-led innovation to Dunkin' Brands, owner of Dunkin' Donuts, allowing Dunkin' to compete successfully against Starbucks on one end and McDonald's on the other.

I did not use a scientific system to pick these folks. They have consistently been multi-sport athletes. They've innovated and succeeded over and over again—but more important, over time. There are a lot more of these decathletes. Another is Joe Tripodi, a marketer who changed businesses by creating value with MasterCard's "Priceless" campaign, Allstate's "Good Hands Guarantee," and the first-ever loyalty program at Coke. Or Gary Loveman, who reinvented the casino industry by leveraging insights, strategy, data, and operational excellence. Or Howard Schultz, who created Starbucks … and then came back and recreated it again. Marketing Decathletes are people who create value for their customers and thereby consistently create value for their businesses. They understand what their businesses need to do to be distinct and differentiated. They are media and channel agnostic. They are brutal. They worship results, and the only people they report to are their customers. They don't all have the same skills or backgrounds. They excel at multiple disciplines because their guiding principle, their North Star, is to deliver value to their customers as no one else can.

CRUSHING THE TEN "EVENTS" OF THE MARKETING DECATHLON

My picks for Marketing Decathletes should have given you a pretty good idea why that old adage about being a jack-of-all-trades and a master of none doesn't really apply in our world today. Becoming a master of one sport—or trade—means that you've not spent time building a solid foundation in the broad range of skills required to survive today. Ironically, a specialist—i.e., a master of one—is at risk of falling behind the jack-of-all-trades, who may not be a star in one sport but who can solidly crush all ten. The jack-of-all-trades is robust, he's rounded, and he doesn't need a party trick—like a gold medal in a single, specific event—to prove his boundless worth. So if you're a specialist, read the ten sections below and see how quickly you can improve at the eight or nine in which you may not be proficient. If you're Jack, make sure that the trades you know are the ones I have identified and described. Enjoy!

Strategic Ability

Above all else, a decathlete understands that strategy is the fundamental capability that separates him or her from the rest of the pack. A business strategy (and therefore a marketing strategy) that truly solves a business's problem by addressing customers' needs in a distinct way is very difficult for marketers who just rely on creative ideas and promotional gimmicks. Developing a compelling strategy results in a focused commitment of all the business resources to an idea that will far outpace "innovations" like a social media campaign or a successful promotion. A strategic approach will finish ahead of even the most attention-grabbing Super Bowl ad, without question, every time.

This is because programs grounded in solid strategic thinking genuinely offer a distinct value proposition to customers, whereas flashy advertising campaigns may or may not connect with audiences. And a decathlete is nothing if not relevant; he's always focused on getting through to the core customers with propositions of value. John Costello realized that Sears was not attracting customers to its soft-goods departments (think apparel), although many of their customers loyally bought Die Hard batteries, Craftsman tools, and Kenmore appliances. Costello had entire floors of inventory to move that had nothing to do with the garage. He knew there was a segment of the market who needed the soft goods to help run their households just as much as their better halves needed tools to tinker with on the weekend, so he invested in a communications strategy that really drove the point home: "The Softer Side of Sears." This move was strategic partly because the soft-goods department was where the bigger profit margins were to be had. Costello put his mouth where the money was—and the customers listened.

The thing about strategic marketers is that they're never just one-hit wonders. When you're dealing with a true Marketing Decathlete, the successes keep coming because they're rooted in sustainable strategic discipline, rather than one-off shots in the dark. At Dunkin'

Donuts, Costello is bringing that same strategic thinking to bear. This is inarguably a high-volume business; I don't think there's anyone out there who would argue that Dunkin' Donuts can't get people through the door (or the drive-through). You've seen the lines in the morning, right? So Costello knows that's not the business problem he needs to solve.

He realized that Dunkin' Donuts, like Sears, had faithful customers. The question was how to hold onto those loyal customers while inducing non-loyalists to stop by and give Dunkin' Donuts a shot. Costello has a deep understanding of his customers, and he delivers innovation consistently. His innovation for Dunkin' was to introduce new breakfast sandwiches, premium donuts, and other offerings that increased the size of each ticket, making the business more profitable and driving the bottom line up, and up, and up.

In this economy, CMOs can no longer survive by spearheading marketing tactics alone, but rather must incorporate *strategic* marketing grounded on a specific, strategic platform that connects the customer to the business by addressing real needs in a compelling and distinct way.

There's an important distinction to make here: In no way should this anecdote be interpreted as a license to indiscriminately inundate your customers with new offerings. A good counter-example is McDonald's, which has been dealing with challenges caused by its decision to significantly increase its menu offerings over the past decade—an action that was completely counter to its core business and operating model.

When McDonald's saw that its customers were demanding healthier options and were therefore visiting "healthier" places like Chipotle for lower calorie counts, it moved in exactly the *wrong* direction. Its solution was to drastically expand the menu, launching new products like salads and wraps. What was once a simple value proposition—good food at a good value, made quickly—became needlessly complicated.

The power of simplicity is one of the basic foundations of any strategy. Successful marketers understand that at a fundamental level, any business delivers a simple solution to a customer's problem. John understands this. As he said in an interview in *Forbes*, "The basic principle to everything we do, especially in the area of communications, is simplicity." [1] If McDonald's had applied this principle, it would have focused on its core products, making them healthier, while keeping the operating model simple—and its success would have continued. A good lesson to learn.

Creative Energy

Focusing on strategy doesn't mean you have to ignore out-of-the-box solutions. It just means that you have to be methodical about how you approach those solutions. It might seem like a contradiction in terms, but a decathlete has to straddle these two worlds—the creative and the strategic—and integrate them into a powerful approach to boosting business.

Particularly since the advent of television advertising, creativity has been a big buzzword in our industry. Everyone wants an ad

---

1 "Dunkin's CMO John Costello Shares His Recipe for Growth." *Forbes*. March 25, 2012. Accessed July 25, 2015.

campaign that makes a splash. We have award shows like the Cannes Lions, the Clios, the One Club's One Show Interactive awards, and others that recognize and reward creativity. On the other hand, we've got awards like the Effies and the Direct Marketing Association's Echo Awards, which champion performance, measuring the impact of campaigns on business performance.

It's too bad that many people see these two approaches as mutually exclusive, when really the approach should be more like a Venn diagram, with the intersection being where we all should want to land. The reality is that in today's world, no matter how fun and flashy an ad campaign might be, if it doesn't convince your customers to do what you want them to do, then you've just made art for no reason. And as CMOs, a big portfolio of beautiful art with no action just isn't going to get contracts re-upped when it comes time to face the board, who are looking for the ringing sound of the cash registers.

Creative, impactful marketing campaigns should resonate at a personal level in a way that convinces your customer to buy your product again and again and recommend that product to others. A campaign should turn the awareness you've created into actual sales. Marketing Decathletes don't just settle for award-winning campaigns; they strive for programs that help their brands grow their share and bring profitable growth to their businesses. By ensuring that campaigns perform the dual functions of creating awareness and generating revenue, they are constructing propositions that will make it in the long haul, rather than just the sprint.

But back to how to get creativity *right*. Cecilia McKenney (who, remember, is *not* from a marketing background) was instrumental in developing perhaps the most effective advertising campaign in Frontier Communications' history. She did this by thinking creatively about how to communicate Frontier's core ethos to its core customers—middle-class Americans who live in rural areas and smaller communities. They want good, transparent service that doesn't get lost in the fine print. With help from her agency, she created Frank the Buffalo, which, in conjunction with Frontier's tagline, "You can't get BS from a buffalo," made for an attention-grabbing campaign that stayed true to Frontier's value proposition of transparent, customer-focused telecom. "We chose Frank because, as an American buffalo, he's classic, true-blue America, just like Frontier," explains the company's website in its humorous but genuine "Frank Facts" section.

Digital Awareness

These days, everyone has something to say about the world of digital. Most people (boards, CEOs, the media) always seem to be pushing us to jump on the latest digital fad, trend, or bandwagon. But here's the thing about decathlete marketers: Those who embraced the digital world early did so for good reason; those who waited eventually embraced it for its strategic benefit, *not* because they were succumbing to peer pressure. The thing about true visionaries—and most of those true visionaries are decathletes, rather than one-sport athletes—is that they are immune to tricks and trends. Rather, they are interested in tools that will help them deliver on their promise. And it should be noted that they don't perceive newness as a threat. They stay open-minded, they investigate, and if the time and the cause are right, they act.

The decathletes who embraced digital didn't try to use digital platforms to build up loyalty or feel-good vibes or the halo effect or whatever you want to call it (we'll talk about this in greater detail in the next chapter). Instead, they embraced digital as an enabler of exponentially bigger ideas that create exponentially greater business impact. Like the decathletes we talked about in the previous section on creativity, decathletes who understand digital use it as a strategic platform with which to address business problems, developing applications and tools with real ROI potential, rather than smoke and mirrors.

I provided a brief account of how Michael Grasso leveraged the power of digital technology to deliver a highly innovative solution that reshaped the commoditized energy marketplace in Texas. Here's what he did: He led the development of a smart-meter-friendly solution called the *TXU Energy MyEnergy Dashboard*[SM], a tool that helped TXU customers understand how and when they use electricity in their homes. It showed them their electricity usage at home, within the context of outdoor temperatures, and it showed them their usage and billing trends over time. Available to all TXU customers for free, this digital tool helped customers examine how and when they used electricity so that they could reduce their energy consumption and, ultimately, their monthly bills. It was the first solution of its kind in Texas, and it provided the real-world benefits of smart meter technology to TXU customers.

Customers used this information to make decisions about their usage and choice of electricity plans, which helped them save energy and lower their costs. The data allowed TXU to automatically generate dashboards for customers when they logged in to txu.com/myaccount, complementing customized at-home guidance provided through Brighten^{SM} Personal Energy Advisor, a free energy-saving solution that offered personalized tips and how-to videos that helped them avoid wasting energy via air leaks, faulty thermostats, insufficient insulation, water heater settings, HVAC inefficiency, and more.

Additionally, the Brighten^{SM} iThermostat empowered customers by providing them with hands-on access to their real-time HVAC settings from virtually anywhere. It allowed them to track and monitor estimated heating and cooling costs, customize daily indoor temperature, and change thermostat settings using their mobile devices.

Grasso didn't stop there. He launched a new mobile website that connected TXU customers with their electricity accounts via Web-enabled wireless devices, making TXU the first retail electricity provider in Texas—and one of the first in the U.S.—to offer its customers optimized mobile access to their accounts to view and pay bills. All this took place a few years before mobile banking became a reality.

The customer comes first with every Marketing Decathlete. As Michael Grasso said in an interview, "At TXU Energy, we continue to raise the bar to provide the most positive customer experience we can, and this innovation is our latest enhancement to fit our customers' always-on, on-the-go lifestyles." This is why decathletes do what they do.

Data Facility

As one might expect, data and digital go hand in hand. Data predates digital—just take a look at the floors of files any good consumer-products company has of all their research. But digital is now making data more valuable by making it easily available and easily understandable. The hype over "big data" is hard to ignore, but smart decathletes have understood the power of data from the very beginning. They've also understood when data has been nothing more than a mirage.

If we return to the forest-versus-tree metaphor, the thing that decathletes have that one-sport wonders don't is a view of the *entire* forest. They don't get caught up on one aspect of data—or one tree— that happens to be right in front of them. They understand that the overall meaning gleaned from data depends on the *context*—that big picture. They developed this understanding long before computing power made it possible for all sorts of people to collect, cull, and categorize all sorts of data—not just the people trained to decipher the data. Decathletes understand that to harness the power of data and parlay it into strategic maneuvers, they must do three things:

First, decathletes *interrogate the data.* They don't just collect big piles of it and fall into the blue-sky trap—that popular methodology of letting every observation bubble up from all the available data. As I have seen in almost every such instance, all you get are generic insights. Decathletes aren't on the hunt for generic insights—they want specific and powerful insights that will inspire ideas that drive sustainable sales. They begin with an end in mind. All the information they gather is meant to find answers to precise questions that can help them solve specific problems.

Second, decathletes connect (and contrast) actual customer behaviors with what they have learned about the beliefs of those customers. They don't just rely on research and claimed data; they cross-check these answers against real-world behaviors so that the resultant strategy can be put into action. They realize that in a majority of categories, they will find dissonance between what their customers believe and how they behave. They don't ignore this dissonance between what they *say* they would do and what they *actually* do, but use this as a crux of their strategic posture.

Finally, decathletes understand how to *structure the gathering of and response to data in an actionable way*. Most non-decathletes have a tendency to get caught up in the analysis-paralysis trap. They get so caught up in all the data that can be generated that they either test everything (whether or not it has any significant impact) or they just begin to ignore the data and use the old-fashioned "hunch" approach. Decathletes make their data efforts meaningful. They collect and use only what they need to make actionable decisions and to develop significant innovations.

Tom O'Toole's work on the United Mileage Plus Program shows us how decathletes succeed by utilizing data. Instead of taking an unfocused approach and drowning in a sea of data, O'Toole used the data to create compelling experiences for his very best customers—a tier called Global Services. His actions addressed his customers' needs for seamless travel, recognition, and comfort—resulting in clearly identified boarding lines, special bag ID wraps, automatic inclusion in the TSA Pre✓® security program, and so on. It was targeted, it was actionable, and it was a success.

Innovative Mindset

No doubt about it, regardless of his or her position in the company, a decathlete is always one of the most innovative people in the building. Whether he's the CMO or the head of HR, a decathlete can't help but innovate—and not just as an attention-grabbing ploy. Innovative decathletes are always thinking about how to solve the problems of their businesses or the problems of their customers (and really, the two, in their minds, are intimately tied together; it's the core value proposition, after all).

Innovators develop new ideas and capabilities that will facilitate marketing, rather than marketing for marketing's sake. Just as Grasso used innovative technology to create a service that responded to his customers' need to spend less on energy, just as O'Toole created innovations in the loyalty program that made a real difference in the United traveler's experience, these innovators are solving real, fundamental problems for their core customers. They're not just telling their customers what they want to hear and hoping they can keep those promises. Real innovators go deeper than that. They put their money where their mouths are—and only then can they put their money into marketing.

Customer-centricity

Because decathletes are masters of focused, actionable strategy, they are focused on their core customers first and foremost. You won't find a decathlete lifting a finger to create, tweak, or promote anything for anyone but the absolute core customer. Those core customers have bull's-eyes painted on their wallets; they are strategic value targets, and the decathlete knows that they are the ones who will give the business the most revenue and the most profit.

In business, there's a well-known rule called the Pareto Principle. Simplified, this rule states that 80 percent of sales will come from 20 percent of a business's clients. Traditional marketers look at this statistic and bemoan the fact that they're leaving this four-fold larger (20% x 4 = 80%) customer base untapped. Trained to prospect, they resort to desperate tricks to woo those customers. If they feel their untapped customer is price-sensitive, they'll race to the bottom with prices. If they feel their untapped customer wants something that's completely out of their wheelhouse, they'll dive into a product segment with which they're tragically unfamiliar (earlier in this chapter we talked about how McDonald's did this).

My firm conducted a study in which we looked at customer-level profitability for fifty of the top consumer-products companies. We found that 19 percent of these companies' top customers deliver 197 percent of their profits. The bottom 30 percent *lose* them 97 percent of this profit, while the remaining 51 percent in the middle break even. Interestingly, even though this 19 percent were their best and most profitable customers, they still had enough headroom to deliver three-to-five times more growth. Marketing Decathletes understand this. That is why they focus all their thinking, innovation, and muscle into making these core customers happier and more bonded to their brands and businesses. This is in direct contrast to the traditional marketer, who focuses his energies on trying to acquire new consumers, and the response marketer, who focuses on making less valuable customers more valuable.

Mobility at the Center

Just as our fearless decathletes weren't scared to go into digital and data early, they immediately recognized the power of mobility and how it could change their businesses for the better. They're tuned in to the fact that in a few years, we won't be carrying laptops—that the tablet, or a hybrid laptop-tablet-phone, will be the go-to device for everyone. The decathletes see that this will change the way customers shop, compare, learn, buy, engage, and experience, and they're moving into that space faster than their competition. When Grasso engineered the mobile apps to control the thermostat, he was the first in the utility space to do so. O'Toole has created fantastic mobile apps to enhance the travel experience with United; on a recent flight from Newark to Mumbai for a conference, I was able to change my seat from my phone when I saw there was a more comfortable one open a few rows behind me!

Unfortunately for McKenney and Frontier, this is one area where they haven't made progress. They could easily create an app much like Uber's that would allow customers to view, in real time, where Frontier's service associate is during the time window provided. Gone would be the days of having to stay home from work for a four-hour window while you wait for your cable guy. It's an investment, to be sure, but it's one that would surely pay dividends. Frontier hasn't done this yet, which shows that not all decathletes are brilliant at all times. But on the whole, decathletes have shown the willingness to move toward mobility as mobility moves the world forward.

Experience Delivery

Decathletes understand that all the areas in which they excel are in the service of improving the customer experience. They understand that building a brand is not solely about building awareness, but about building an *experience*. Howard Schultz wasn't so much selling coffee with Starbucks as he was selling the *experience* of drinking that coffee in a Starbucks store. He offered a great gathering place, a great place to experience coffee. Panera has created a similar environment that goes far beyond sandwiches, soups, and salads: They've got free Wi-Fi®, convenient locations, a fast process, and a quality product. And you can stay there and work the entire day, as I have done occasionally while traveling on business. Retail stores like Williams-Sonoma or Sur La Table have gone beyond simply offering cookware; they have cooking classes and other experiences in the store. Decathletes understand that the creation of an exceptional experience for the *full cycle* of purchase is the only way to build a deeper relationship with their customers today.

Engagement Focus

When you focus on creating a deeper, more fulfilling experience, you are ultimately creating a more engaged relationship with your customer. Your customers will feel not only that you understand them well, but also that you care for them, and that's why you're so responsive to their needs. And that feeling will be genuine, because if you're a decathlete, you *do* care. You understand your core customers, not just as a target or as a decile; you understand them as real people, you understand their needs and desires, and you go far to fulfill them.

We'll go deeper into this when we talk about social media in the next chapter, but one of the ways that brands foster engagement today is by creating communities. One of my favorite examples of this from my own life doesn't come from a blue-chip company like Starbucks, but rather, from a guy named Justin Sandercoe who offers free guitar lessons online at www.justinguitar.com. He's created what amounts to a free music school, with an option to pay for certain features if you choose. He's made the experience very personal for each user; in addition to his advice, his site offers a community that can provide advice and feedback at any time. I bought his Beginner lesson kit a while ago. When I found myself having trouble with a difficult riff, I went to the community page to ask a question and found that I wasn't the only student of Justin's in my town—there were three more of us. One of them, I learned, is a contemporary of mine; we'd met at a fundraiser for my daughter's school choir, in which his daughter also sang.

While Justin has created communities that drive engagement, other brands drive engagement by responding to customers in very visible ways. Another Internet-enabled sensation that does this well is Tom Dickson and his Blendtec® brand of blenders. If you haven't seen the videos, I'd encourage you to take a look at them; quite frankly, they're like nothing you've ever seen before. His YouTube channel asks (and definitively answers) the question: "Will it blend?" Customers can send in requests, and Dickson himself will appear in a lab coat in some kind of mad scientist-run R&D lab, engaging and enthralling customers by blending up iPhones, bricks, two-by-fours, golf balls, you name it. (Bad day on the golf course? Tell Tom, and you might open your browser window to see him giving a bucket of balls an even worse day.) The channel helped drive sales for the private-label brand, ultimately transforming it into a premium brand.

Deliver on Equity

And that's where our last skill set comes in. Decathletes understand that every effort—from advertising to experience to engagement and beyond—has to be grounded on a strategic platform that is connected to the core values of the brand while providing real benefits to their customers. And they have to do this in a way that is true to their values. Authenticity is key. Performance is key. Tom Dickson, then CEO of Blendtec, used to blend wooden boards to test product performance. After Blendtec made this a key part of its marketing efforts, it saw sales increase by over 700 percent[2] while

---

[2] SocialLens Blendtec Case Study, January 2009

improving their brand equity. Shortly before this writing, Dickson sold Blendtec to a private equity firm for an undisclosed sum. I'm willing to bet it wasn't for chump change; he clearly had an affinity for his product, and you don't fork over your life's work for pennies.

The principles he used are the core principles I see other decathletes use regularly:

1. Align your marketing to business and brand strategy. Blendtec's viral videos and their content aligned nicely with its brand of high-quality, technically sophisticated blenders. It also supported its objective to build brand awareness.

2. Be authentic and true. Tom Dickson's charm is not his smooth presentation style. It is his "mad scientist" authenticity. He wasn't just the CEO of a corporation. He was also a guy who was passionate about his products.

3. Engage your core customers. Blendtec sent e-mails to its customer base asking for recommendations for things to blend. It still accepts suggestions via an online form. This open invitation allows the community to participate in the process.

So in Dickson's case, as in the case of Starbucks or Panera or United, you can see that there's a very quantifiable end to all of this, and it's *financial.* In order for these things to go deeper than stunts, in order for them to be sustained, they must have a positive, measurable impact on the financial performance of the business. Splashy apps and ad campaigns and mascots and characters aren't going to stand the test of time if the cash register doesn't ring loudly and often. Ensuring that the equity value in the brand increases concurrently with the equity in the business is the only true way to get into the record books. And when you're a decathlete, those records look all the more impressive.

CHAPTER 4

Where Social, Big Data, IoT, Mobile, and Micro-Segmentation Really Lead (Actually, Nowhere)

IF YOU WANT to talk about some of the biggest culprits in the plague of time starvation, look no further than the title of this chapter. It seems that every day, there's a new piece of innovation, a new start-up, a new app, a new *something* that cries out for us to take tech and tech-related tactics seriously. Even for the seasoned veterans among us (and I'd argue, perhaps, even *more* so for the seasoned veterans among us), it's getting tough to separate the wheat from the chaff. External and internal pressures make us feel like we have to invest our limited dollars and even more limited time in every new technology and tool that comes along. Social, big data, IoT, mobile, micro-segmentation— these are the buzzwords that the beleaguered CMO is muttering in his sleep in the midst of nightmares and night sweats.

Even before this most recent explosion of options and so-called opportunities, marketers have been dealing with the issue of where to focus their attention and assets. This has been going on since the mid-1990s, when the Internet went from cool gadget to game-changer. I can still remember the long hours we spent discussing the potential and value of this new ... we weren't sure—medium, channel, or thing. The conversations escalated as data-driven and tech-first businesses such as retailers and financial-services providers got into e-commerce and began using this channel and the value it created to refine their business models, while consumer-packaged goods companies (P&G and Kraft, for instance) were hanging back and asking questions: *Should we embrace the Internet? If so, what should we do with it? What role can it play in our marketing?*

All in all, hindsight being twenty-twenty, I think their hesitation at that time was smart. Before these traditional brand-oriented marketers jumped headlong into the Internet game, they waited to learn and understand what the role of that game would be, and in turn, what *their* part would be as the game evolved. This pause for introspection was a smart move. It allowed them to understand that during the early and mid-phases of the development and adoption of the Internet, the products they sold were not e-commerce oriented. They did see that the Internet enabled the development of credible social outlets, and as these outlets evolved into robust, consumer-led ecosystems, they were able to use these to build experiences that drove engagement for their brands. This allowed them to take back control of their disintermediated end-customer relationships from the retailers.

Dana Anderson, another Marketing Decathlete, has been using these emerging channels to turn old staples like Oreos into knock-out successes. In her role as SVP of brand marketing at Kraft, and then as CMO at Kraft's spin-off company, Mondelēz, she helped transform a very traditional marketing culture into a nimble, start-up mindset by forcing people to look at new ways to connect brands with their customers.

The Oreo renaissance is one of many such wins. "You can still dunk in the dark": This Oreo tweet during the 2014 Super Bowl blackout was the talk of the marketing world for months. At this year's SXSW, the brand created a 3–D cookie printer to dispense customized treats. It has sponsored Snack Hacks, which shows innovative ways to dunk an Oreo cookie in milk via six-second Vine videos. Recently, it has launched a program celebrating "small" by giving packages of Oreo Minis to people whose small gestures have made a big impact.

Dana has been an advocate for extraordinary quality and relevance in advertising. She's also managed to embrace the new world with apparent ease, while constantly challenging convention—and sometimes big convention. She characterizes today's marketing dynamic as the reduction of time and the expansion of channels through digital means. (She often says that "digital just didn't make one new channel—it created thousands of new mediums.") This has created a new way of working with a diverse group of contributors who can thrive amid change and chaos. Her core belief that "creativity in all of its forms is vital to consumers, so it's vital to us [marketers]" is the guidepost that has made her successful—and it will make *all* marketers successful if they stay committed to it. She has made a huge impact in today's changing environment, and so can you.

If you've any doubt, let it go, because now the future is ... well, *now!* We are in the eye of this storm. The torrent of different technologies, the deluge of data (big data is already sinking under the weight of its expectations), and the infatuation with new techniques will continue to vex marketers and customers alike, because we're in an era of unprecedented hype. Every new idea, every new app, every new product, every new toy, and every new fad seems to get blown up and out of proportion. No one can predict what's going to stick, and no one wants to miss out if something does, so everyone wants to be involved in everything. This makes it difficult for marketers today. How do you begin to drown out all the noise and really focus on what's going to work for you?

A DOSE OF HEALTHY SOCIAL MEDIA SKEPTICISM

Believe me when I say that I'm not afraid of change. I appreciate the value of trying new things—maybe more than the next guy. But I've found that one of the best ways to keep from falling off a cliff is to look before I leap. Marketers today would do well to follow this simple advice, particularly if they want to avoid getting lost in the churn of an era of fickle fads.

Looking back to the late '90s, long after the question of whether to embrace the Internet had ceased to be a topic of discussion (the verdict, obviously, was yes, it was here to stay), I remember speaking about the future of brands and marketing at the National Retail Federation's annual meeting in New York. At the time, social media was waiting in the wings, not yet standard, but starting to percolate. Reuters had sent a reporter out to cover predictions and reactions to social media from senior retail marketers at the meeting; he'd been hearing all day from every thought leader that "social was the next big thing, and that if you weren't already doing it, you were going to lose." When he called me for my thoughts, I'm sure he was expecting more of the same. We ended up having a fascinating conversation about my reasons for disagreeing.

It wasn't that I didn't think social media was important, or that it wasn't a valuable part of the future of marketing; it's just that I believed that the social channel was not just a marketing ploy. It needed to be a high-priority business initiative. Why? Social channels for the first time allowed consumers and customers to have direct, real-time access to companies, 24/7. This, therefore, required companies to have infrastructure and processes in place to respond in real time. Very few companies had this infrastructure at that time. My assertion was that without this infrastructure, companies were setting themselves up to damage their relationships with those customers who attempted to connect and were unsuccessful. None of us likes an unanswered contact.

It was interesting to see that I was the only nay-sayer in that group. All others were exhorting marketers to jump on this bandwagon. Social media gurus were springing up everywhere you looked, and there was no shortage of them. That's the thing about fads: No one wants to be left behind, especially when they're so enticing. My argument that social media was fundamentally different from traditional media was a lost sound in the wilderness. I felt that companies that looked at social media as just a media channel—the same as their print channels or television spots—were setting themselves up for a very rude awakening. Social media opened a direct line to consumers; it gave them the ability to connect and communicate with companies in real time. And most companies didn't have the infrastructure in place to deal with the consequences of this. With a technology this new, it would be pretty much impossible to have that kind of infrastructure in place right off the bat. And without a collaborative model to enable them to listen and respond instantaneously, some of them found themselves in a whole world of trouble.

SOCIAL FLOPS AND FAUX PAS

Now, more than a decade in, we've learned a lot about how to handle (and how *not* to handle) social media. We've learned much from companies that were very successful in their own right but faltered when it came to handling the double-edged sword of social activism.

Remember, for instance, when United Airlines customer and musician Dave Carroll's guitar was broken on a United flight in 2008? If it had happened in an earlier time, you probably wouldn't; thanks to YouTube, however, you probably do. Here's the story in case you don't: A singer/songwriter named Dave Carroll was flying from Halifax, Nova Scotia, to Omaha, Nebraska, with a layover at Chicago's O'Hare airport. As he was getting ready to get off the plane, he heard another passenger say, "My God! They're throwing guitars out there!" As Dave and the other band members looked out onto the tarmac, where the luggage was being unloaded, they recognized their guitars. Their reaction was a blend of horror and disbelief. Later he discovered that the neck of his $3,500 Taylor guitar had been broken.

What followed was a customer-service nightmare. Dave tried for nine months to get a claim processed with United. The response was a firm and consistent "no." The company claimed he had waited longer than 24 hours to process a claim, so he was out of luck. He tried phone calls. He tried e-mails. He even went so far as to suggest that instead of money, United give him $1,200 in flight vouchers to cover the cost of repairing the guitar.

United held firm. It said no. So what could a singer-songwriter do? He wrote a song and produced a music video. The song was titled "United Breaks Guitars." He put it up on YouTube and it went viral. Very soon thereafter, large numbers of people were singing along to "United Breaks Guitars." The video was posted on July 6, 2009. It amassed 150,000 views within one day, prompting United to contact Carroll and offer to right the wrong. The video had garnered over half a million hits by July 9, 5 million by mid-August 2009, 10 million by February 2011, and 14 million by February 2015.

After 150,000 views, United contacted Dave Carroll and offered payment to make the video go away. He had changed his mind, however. It wasn't about the money anymore. In fact, he suggested that United donate the money to a charity. Here's the kicker: Within four days of the video being posted online, United Airlines' stock price fell 10 percent, costing stockholders about $180 million in value. An expensive lesson, wouldn't you say?

Bud Light had to deal with a similar issue. In late April 2015, negative comments began flooding social media following extensive news coverage of a marketing message printed on some bottles that some critics said could be interpreted as contributing to a "rape culture." These bottles were emblazoned with a slogan proclaiming Bud Light to be "the perfect beer for removing 'no' from your vocabulary for the night." The brew's "buzz" score fell from six to zero in fewer than three days, according to the YouGov BrandIndex, which measures daily brand consumer perception. The average score for domestic beers is currently 4, putting Bud Light below its peers. Among women, Bud Light fell from a 5 to –3. "The drop that we are seeing is statistically significant. It is meaningful," said Ted Marzilli, CEO of YouGov BrandIndex.

The power that social media places in the hands of consumers shouldn't be underestimated, as United and Bud Light learned; the ramifications can mean real losses in real dollars. Whereas marketers have been hard-pressed to show specific ROI from social media, there is certainly no shortage of examples of the power of social channels to lower the bottom line. Gap and Tropicana spent *millions* on new packaging and new logos, only to have to scramble after social media backlash forced them to scrap the designs and go back to the drawing board with their tails between their legs. It's a one-two punch: The first blow comes when the grumbling starts, and the knockout gets delivered when companies can't (or don't) respond in real time to that grumbling, which soon becomes a deafening roar.

What can we take away from all of this, other than a healthy respect for looking before we leap? We can certainly say, based on these and other examples, that social media isn't just a marketing issue. Instead, it has to be managed as a critical *business* function. The entire enterprise must be behind the social strategy—how it's implemented, how it's monitored, and how it's used. Then and only then can you rest assured that you've got a fair chance to succeed in this brave new world.

THE TRUTH ABOUT FADS

Some fads burn out quickly; that's why they're fads. Remember QR codes? The RFID chip? On the other hand, there are success stories: Facebook, Twitter, LinkedIn; the list goes on. These are tools that clearly are here to stay. Now that social media has asserted itself, it seems that everyone has moved on to big data.

What to make of big data? Is it a fad like the QR code, or is it something that's truly indispensable and will become a standard, like a presence on Facebook or LinkedIn?

I'd argue that there's a more important issue at hand: that the questions we're asking about big data should be less speculative about its place in the annals of marketing history (or marketing's future) and more focused on what big data can—or can't—actually do for us. Does big data lead to big payoffs?

My sense is that in most cases, it doesn't. No matter what kind of spin you put on it, a pile of big data the size of the Great Pyramid isn't going to amount to the financial relevance of an anthill if it isn't contextualized properly. And for the most part, the big data that's out there isn't. I'd guess that only about 5 percent (if that) is truly useful, or even structured so that marketers and companies can use it effectively. Just having the data doesn't mean much; whether we can use it without a gargantuan amount of effort is the key question.

I, for one, understand the pull fads have on the consumer, to say nothing of the marketer. I always had to be the first in line; I was an early adopter of almost every new technology—including disasters like Apple's Newton—and I was the first to get the first-ever flip phone, Motorola's StarTAC (which I helped launch). But I've found, both in business and in life, that sometimes there are benefits to waiting a little bit before diving into new technology.

Now, don't get me wrong—I got the Apple Watch as soon as it was available, so what I'm going to state is not blanket but directional. With technology changing as quickly as it does today, rather than committing my time and money to be what amounts to a beta test, I've learned to hang back a little bit. It's not because I've gotten older, or lost my capacity to deal with new technology. It's also not because I'm afraid of change. It is because I've realized that I should be more discerning about the time, energy, and money that I invest in the new technologies. Now I use a simple litmus test: Is it really going to make a difference in my life and add another (positive) dimension to the way I do things? If yes, then by all means, I'll jump right in. But if it's not going to make my life better, I can afford to wait a while.

There are three primary reasons for this. The first is, like everyone else, I'm dealing with the issue of time starvation. Given all the pressures that I have in my personal and professional life, I don't have the time to get caught up in fads, to fall down rabbit holes. And this logic extends to my professional role as a marketer as well as my personal role as a consumer. In Chapter Two, when we discussed CMOs not being able to see the forest for the trees, this is precisely the issue I was talking about: The more you let yourself become eclipsed by swiftly rotating fads, the less you're going to be able to see the big picture. I also have limited resources in terms of time and budget; this is no small thing, either for the consumer or for the CMO. And finally, I have a limited attention span. I can't send myself chasing so many different things and expect to reach the finish line with any reasonable expediency.

WHY BIG DATA AND MICRO-SEGMENTATION *AREN'T* CURE-ALLS

Looking at big data and micro-segmentation under the critical microscope of the *selective* and *skeptical* (note: not *scared*) early adopter, we can start to see how fads that initially look shiny and perfect often lose their luster upon closer inspection. Amazon has been one of the power users of data and technology to make shopping for literally anything easy. This was its strategy: Delivering great customer experiences and providing its customers with anything and everything they want and need. Amazon has done this incredibly well for a long time and has benefited from this level of focus on its customers.

However, of late, customers and reviewers have begun to see cracks in its foundation. As Panos Mourdoukoutas wrote in *Forbes* in October 2014, "For years, Amazon has been obsessed with growth, in all directions, building warehouses and distribution centers, video stream services, and mobile devices—to mention but a few of those directions. And in a big shift from Amazon.com's long-standing business model—which has relied on online sales and remote warehouses to compete effectively against major discount retailers like Walmart—the company is to open its first physical store on 34th Street in Manhattan, across from the Empire State Building. But a recent survey of Amazon's prime customers showed a big decline in membership would occur should Amazon raise the price of its service. Simply put, in spite of its size, Amazon.com cannot take the customer for granted. [The company] doesn't have pricing power because it has pitted [itself] against giants in every area into which [it has] expanded its presence. In the meantime, the company has been expanding its subscription customer base by keeping the price for its products and services low. That's how it amassed close to $82 billion in revenues at razor thin margins."

Amazon is an amazing company, and the assertion I'm making is counterintuitive for many people, but I believe it to be true. Let me begin with a confession: I'm one of Amazon's best customers. I buy almost everything I need from them, including content.

I'm also the author of *Brand Rituals,* the book Amazon keeps recommending to me, and I'm the owner of several other books, music CDs, gizmos, and gadgets that I've bought *from* Amazon, and which Amazon continues to suggest that I purchase. I'm the owner of a Kindle filled with e-books from the Kindle store, which are also then recommended to me by Kindle, sometimes within days of my purchase. It's easy to see how the timing of activities is not synchronous anymore—the predictive algorithms often guess correctly the things that I would be interested in, but the technology doesn't have the intelligence to interrogate that data, to get to the *why.* It can't discriminate between my interest in something and my previous actions.

So what's going on here? Is it just that the technology isn't ready for what we want it to do? Maybe. But there's something that goes deeper than just a technical issue, and again, the problem is rooted in the fact that one can only have so much attention, so much time, and so much money. To stick with the Amazon example, the expansion of the Amazon brand into all of these different areas has exponentially increased the issue of time and attention starvation for them. What was once purely a retail brand built on operational excellence has now become a consumer-products company (selling Fire, Kindle, tablets, etc.). It has also become a media company (music, video, books, publications, proprietary shows, etc.). Amazon Web Services offers a broad set of global computing, storage, database, analytics, application, and deployment services that help organizations move faster, reduce IT costs, and scale applications, putting it squarely into business services.

With all these expansions, the company's ability to connect all the dots to serve me as proactively and as well as it did in the past has diminished. In its most basic sense, it's simply *too much information.* The data in each ecosystem can't be cross-referenced, and eventually the left hand doesn't know what the right is doing, leading to deterioration in the experience and subsequent loss of its differentiation.

As we see from the above example, data plays a crucial role. However, the bigger the data gets, the harder it becomes to make it work using the traditional approaches. Letting data blue-sky to find connections and insights no longer works. Too much data just delivers broad and generic observations. To get to insights, you need to actually interrogate data, and do it within the context of your desired business outcomes. I'm not saying that we shouldn't be excited by the capability that comes with big data or micro-segmentation, but I am *absolutely* saying that you can't let yourself get so caught up in rhetoric that you forget what problem you're really trying to solve. By all means, get excited by technology; it's going to enable so much change, and change is exciting. But getting caught up in overhyped solutions will ultimately create more problems than those solutions can address.

These issues aren't unique to Amazon; they're happening all across the market in almost every company in almost every sector. One of the issues is our fascination with fads. Another issue is the fact that due to the media attention, CEOs and boards of companies are becoming enablers of fragmentation. Most CMOs I know are constantly distracted by demands from their bosses and their boards to investigate and experiment with new technologies they learned about in another boardroom. CMOs are given mandates without regard to the appropriateness of those technologies to their business or market position; a smaller, regional player may find itself in over its head trying to execute the same experiment as a big gun like Procter & Gamble with a fraction of the funds available to P&G.

SPINNING YOUR (HAMSTER) WHEELS
VS. GAINING REAL TRACTION

If these forays into folly were just momentary distractions, that would be one thing. But the reality is that once these projects start, they very rarely stop before they've progressed into full-on wheel-spinning operations. It's like the supposedly innocuous hamster that I let my kids bring home from the pet store a few years ago. This one act swiftly metastasized. We got the hamster cage, but then we realized we needed a hamster wheel. Then there were pleas for a second hamster; the first one seemed so lonely in there, after all. Before I knew it, we were stuck with an entire family of hamsters that seemed to do nothing but reproduce with uncanny speed.

If you've ever helmed one of these experimental projects, you know I'm not exaggerating. I've seen it happen time and time again. I see CMOs and their teams drowning in these so-called world-changing innovations, which start to balloon like hamster families. Every few months, another Big Thing gets added, and by the end of each year, marketing plans have artifacts of numerous experiments going nowhere.

You'll never get anywhere other than Burnoutsville this way—and that's a trip without a return ticket. I'm not saying you can't use social media and other tactical projects to your advantage, but the key is that in order for those projects to change the business, they must be fundamentally connected to a core strategic driver of the business. The decathlete marketer is strategic in all things, and technology trends are no exception. Look again to the example of Blendtec, which increased its sales exponentially with a dedicated social campaign. What separates Blendtec from the flashes in the social media pan? Ultimately, Blendtec succeeded because its campaign was based on its *core strategic value proposition* and linked very authentically to a solution that resonated with its customers. Blendtec wanted its customers to know they were getting a great blender, and it spared no expense (or two-by-fours) in creating content that delivered that message quickly and honestly.

And this, decathletes-in-training, is perhaps the most singularly valuable key to cutting through the commotion and connecting with focused, strategic initiatives that really help you gain traction. If you stay focused on the one real problem that you as a brand or product are solving for your consumers, if you can clearly articulate your strategic proposition, everything else will fall into place. That's when you can say goodbye to the hamster wheel.

SEARCHING FOR SIGNIFICANCE

In all of this, if I were to tease out another key point (other than the necessity for strategy to ground each and every action, no matter how tried and tested or technologically advanced), it would be that we should ensure that all actions result in statistically significant outcomes.

Most new-world marketing gurus seem to push the softer and non-revenue-oriented measures to a number of new marketing fads. Yes, we need to be present and approachable, but we also need to be accountable. Be careful of the hamsters, fellow CMOs. Just because a new-world approach is cool and different doesn't mean that it has the ability to deliver significant business impact.

When I launched my last book, *Brand Rituals: How Successful Brands Bond with Customers for Life*, one of the first places I went to present it was the Direct Marketing Educational Foundation's annual event. I've been in the business a long time, but I still look at this event as something of a marketing classroom experience; the top leaders from the Direct Marketing industry gather under one roof to share what they're up to and what they've learned.

Because I arrived well before my presentation, I was able to catch some of the earlier presentations. One that stuck with me was a case study about the use of segmentation and CRM techniques to increase purchase of Kraft products. The speaker talked about how Kraft was leveraging the database it had built to gain insight into its consumers. As you might imagine, the Kraft database was quite vast; it claimed to have data on more than 16 million households that they analyzed and harnessed to execute an e-mail marketing campaign. Again, as you might imagine, the program sounded quite impressive ... until it came to the results. It seems Kraft enjoyed a $12 million spike in incremental revenue, which it attributed to conversions from this program. I guess it provided a good lesson, but for a company with total revenue of over $18 billion, this incremental revenue gain isn't even a proverbial drop in the bucket.

The moral of the story: If you're searching for significance—statistical or otherwise—I'd encourage you not to pay too much attention to fads. Look at ideas that will become trends. In this economy of today, this Insight Economy, the real success stories are coming from companies that don't get caught up in looking for the silver bullet. The marketers who succeed are the ones who aren't looking to find the next big thing that's going to help them achieve a breakthrough. They've got something far steadier, and far more sustainable. They've got a North Star pointing them toward the right finish line. No matter where they go, no matter how tough the going gets, they look to that North Star and know that every decision they make leading in that direction will be the right one.

What is that North Star? Your best and most loyal customer.

CHAPTER 5

From the Attention Economy to Attention Deficit Disorder: How Even Great Companies Got Lost in the Transition to the Insight Economy

IN TURBULENT TIMES, many people grasp for stability and structure by adhering to rules they learned early in life. This makes sense; it's how we're socialized to behave in our daily lives. After all, chief marketing officers are no different; in many ways, sticking to rules is a way to shield themselves from criticism, as they tell their CEOs and boards, "Look, here's a concrete example of what we're doing. We're doing this the way other category leaders do. This is how things work in our category." We all remember being told, "You'll never get fired for buying IBM or for emulating P&G." These rules made the lives of marketers quite easy for a while.

But what if things change, and the rules we follow just *aren't* the rules anymore? This is the problem that has befallen many companies. These companies were unable to manage the transition from the Attention Economy to the Information Economy and now to the Insight Economy. In a world where only the most nimble, flexible Marketing Decathletes are succeeding, one- and two-sport athletes who came of age in the time of traditional marketing models are struggling to keep up.

COMING OF AGE IN THE ATTENTION ECONOMY (CIRCA 1960–1984)

In the Attention Economy, every product launch was a big launch. Think of how Ford would launch a new car—it was a slow, decisive, thorough, and well-researched path from concept to consumer, taking many months if not a couple of years—and you'll understand how things worked in the Attention Economy. There weren't many products and there weren't many segments. Businesses operated in a fairly homogeneous environment, each competing against a small number of similar companies. In fact, only the biggest companies with large advertising and marketing budgets could really afford to launch products successfully, simply because you needed big guns that only the big companies could afford. AMC's show *Mad Men* brought this era to life very well. If you had the money to make a splash with big television and print campaigns, then you had a chance. If not, you were bound to get lost in the spray from the cannonballs. Still, something happened when these companies that came of age in the Attention Economy really started to grow during the next phase of the economy, the Information Economy (circa 1984–2014).

Case Study: McDonald's

The experiences of McDonald's offer a great example of some of the growing pains that have plagued companies during these era transitions. Growing from just a simple roadside operation in 1940 to around five hundred stores in 1963 (the year of my birth), to around 10,000 stores in the late 1980s, McDonald's enjoyed explosive growth that dovetailed with the population boom in the U.S. and around the world. Suburbia was growing, the middle class was growing, and McDonald's was growing with it.

During that time, the ethos of McDonald's (which was reflected in its advertising) was simple: consistency. You knew you could go there to get good food for a good price in a good, clean environment. You knew that each time you walked into a McDonald's, no matter whether it was the one down the block from the office or one on the other side of the world, you could expect similar offerings with a similar and consistent experience. This became even more important to consumers as they became more starved for time with the advent of the Information Economy.

In all that time, despite the explosive growth of the company from the '60s to the '80s, McDonald's only introduced six items to its menu. These items were introduced with the same fanfare a car manufacturer would devote to the release of a new model—a brand unto itself. These six items (the Filet-O-Fish in 1964 , the Big Mac in 1968, the Quarter Pounder in 1972, the Egg McMuffin in 1973, Sundaes in 1978, and Chicken McNuggets in 1983) have been menu staples since their launch and have been drivers of McDonald's growth and popularity over the decades.

But then, as it is wont to do, the world shifted. While McDonald's continued to grow and grow, we moved into the Information Economy, and the singular lens (that fundamental thing: good food, fast, and cheap) through which it viewed the business splintered into a seemingly infinite number of lenses. In the environment that produced discrete segments of consumers based on discrete and specific need states, McDonald's strayed from its roots. Instead of staying focused on its core value proposition, it began to invest in an ever-expanding lineup of consumer segments: people who want to eat healthy, people who want rock-bottom prices, people who want different regional or ethnically-tweaked tastes, and people who want better coffee. Ironically, most of the company's actions were in response to new competitors.

Other brands—not other mega-brands like Burger King or Wendy's, but smaller, more incremental brands like Chipotle, Starbucks, Five Guys, and Red Robin—were all born of the Information Economy, all built to cater to specific needs of specific audience groups. These brands became highly relevant in their customers' lives; they fulfilled a clear, unmet need. Chipotle, for example, fulfills the need for good, natural food, delivered quickly, but with a twist of customization and premium ingredients. Instead of sticking to the root of its dominance, McDonald's decided to compete with these incremental brands by increasing its offerings and trying to appeal to a wide range of consumer segments. It launched salads. It launched wraps. It tried premium sandwiches. It tried its hand at snacks. It introduced upscale coffee and upscale dessert. And in the process, McDonald's stumbled; not only did sales go down, but so did CEO Don Thompson, who was fired in January 2015.

The problem isn't that McDonald's was taking shots in the dark. It had the data that showed that these segments of customers were out there, at scale; the existence of the incremental brands is proof positive of that. The problem lies in the execution, the idea that superficial tactics are as effective as authentic strategy. It would be one thing if McDonald's actually understood in a deep, gut-level way what it means to be a retailer catering to customers who want healthy and organic foods. But it doesn't. The McDonald's experience—the core that its brand is built upon—is giving customers good food for a good price in a good, clean environment. That's it. To make moves that are dissonant to that foundation won't make *anyone* money but will end up costing a lot. It doesn't matter how good the brand's reputation is; if it's not aligned with its authentic operating model, if it doesn't address the customer's needs in a consistent and distinct way, then that customer is going to go elsewhere. By creating losing innovations, a company creates distractions for itself that alienate those core customers it *did* understand in a deep, fundamental way during its rise to success.

Case Study: Circuit City

I first got involved with Circuit City in 1999, when I helped develop the strategy that led to two years of better-than-category growth for the business. I also helped to develop the marketing campaign titled "We're With You." I stayed involved off-and-on with the business until 2006, and I witnessed its 2009 bankruptcy and liquidation from a distance. What a sad ending to a brand that created the consumer-electronics retail category and was featured in Jim Collins's book *Good to Great*.

So what happened? Before Amazon and the Internet, Best Buy

was Circuit City's biggest competitive problem. Best Buy had a clear value proposition, which was defined by its name: The best selection available at the best prices. It was able to deliver on this because it didn't have the cost burden of a commissioned sales force that Circuit City had to carry. This commission structure was what gave Circuit City its competitive advantage. It motivated its salespeople to stay informed on the latest technology and serve customers extremely well. This approach worked well in the Attention Economy, especially before the digital ecosystem made it easy for every consumer to learn about, price-shop, and compare products with a click of a mouse.

As the world evolved into the Information Economy, Circuit City made its fatal error. With the advent of Amazon and other online retailers, the company drew the conclusion that ease of access and cut-rate prices were what its customers needed. Circuit City saw how Amazon was doing things for *its* customers and thought, *If we want to beat Amazon, we have to beat it at its own game.*

Right? Wrong. Circuit City should have stuck to what it was good at: a high-touch model with highly informed, highly motivated salespeople who could make the most out of each personal consumer interaction. Instead, to manage its cost structure, it eliminated the commission sales model and converted to a single hourly pay structure across all its stores. The highly skilled salespeople left for greener pastures, and Circuit City lost its competitive advantage. It forgot that, no matter how much product you have, and no matter how rock-bottom your pricing, at the end of the day you really have to understand what makes your customers choose you over all the other choices available to them. For Circuit City, it was the passion of its employees to help customers find the right electronics for their home. This service could only be delivered, in those days, by knowledgeable sales folk. The chain did attempt to extend this capability through digital tools, but the technology wasn't available, and by then it was a little too little, a little too late.

Case Study: Amazon

Many have pointed to Amazon as the poster child for success in the Information Economy. If we were to look at Amazon at a particular point in time—the heyday of the Information Economy—we could say yes, that's a true statement.

But as McDonald's has shown, just because you are a juggernaut during one era doesn't mean you are immune to the forces of change at work in the transition to the Insight Economy. Amazon needs to continue to reinvent itself, but this needs to be done within the context of the needs its customers want fulfilled and the problems they need solved. And it needs to be done within the context of the customers' expectations of how Amazon will solve their problems. If Amazon is beginning to fall behind in fulfilling these expectations, then it needs to slow down and fix its operating infrastructure before pushing forward to the next stage of growth. If it doesn't, it may become another victim of Information Economy dementia and data overload.

Amazon began with a crystal-clear business model. Simply put, Amazon was the place you could buy anything you wanted, from anywhere in the world, anytime you felt like it. What's more, Amazon gave you the capability to compare prices at lightning speed and to get those items shipped to you lickety-split. Operational excellence leveraging data and technologies formed the foundation that makes this model work. Of late, as detailed earlier, this model is showing some cracks. From its core of uber-retail, to their transition to the Kindle ecosystem, to their move to providing Web services to other businesses, Jeff Bezos has been transforming the giant to make it the one-stop shop for all people for all needs. I believe this is why the customer experience is beginning to weaken, and cracks are becoming evident in Amazon's ability to deliver consistent business results. Although its top line continues to grow, the business has struggled to deliver strong or consistent profits. Since 2011, according to data from Bloomberg Business, with average revenue of $68.15 billion, Amazon has delivered net income of only $625 million. Most other companies that deliver these results would be severely punished by Wall Street, but in Amazon's case, the halo from its success in the Information Economy era provides some insulation. The question is … for how long?

SIMPLE SOLUTIONS IN A COMPLEX WORLD: HOW TO COURSE-CORRECT WITH YOUR CUSTOMER IN MIND

I think we're agreed that we live in a hyper-complex world. It's easy to understand why CMOs and CEOs feel the pressure of market complexity closing in on them. I call this the *curse of the more*; they see *more* data supporting the need to serve *more* customer segments to generate *more* growth resulting in investments in *more* initiatives leading to them diving down *more* rabbit holes.

The solution isn't more complexity. The solution, conceptually, is really simple. So simple, in fact, that most large, sophisticated companies have forgotten about it. So, Zain, what is it? Begin with your customers (not your consumers, not your prospects) in mind. If possible, walk in their shoes. Live their lives for a day, or better yet, a week. Understand their problems and their challenges. Empathize with their joy and sorrow. Get to know them intimately. You'll see that their decisions—what brands to buy and how those brands fit into their lives—are not very complicated. Understanding the role your brand plays in their lives and how you would like to transform that role should be the beginning, middle, and end of all your interactions with them.

Companies that struggled to evolve from the Attention Economy to the Insight Economy missed this one big point. Because they know more and because it is possible to deliver more, they try to do more and end up making their business model *unbelievably* complex. If what they believe the consumer needs is choice, boy, do they give it to them. If I go to Amazon and try to buy a simple shower curtain to match the color scheme of my particular basement bathroom, I'm inundated with over nine hundred thousand options.

This amount of choice isn't just paralyzing for customers, it's also ineffective. Yes, there are tools that allow them to filter and get to the products that they need, but it is still a problem. This is the legacy of the Information Economy; a leveling-up of complexity. Big data, segmented data, gigabytes, terabytes, and petabytes of data, omnichannel, multichannel, I can feel an arrhythmia starting in my chest just typing these words. So I don't blame C-Suite leaders when they lose their ability to think simply and clearly about the consumer's needs.

The marketers who are successfully cutting through the static of the Information Economy and staving off data dementia are the ones who are doing the best job of following the KISS principle— *Keep It Simple, Sir.* They haven't been seduced by mountains of data on each consumer segment. Instead, they are in tune to the fact that they are *serving people.* That's it! Your customers are *people.* They aren't bits and bytes. They are living, breathing human beings with unique behaviors, differing needs, a few idiosyncrasies, and specific problems they need solved.

If you're a marketing veteran, you most likely are saying, "Tell me something I don't know." Here's something: In consulting with seventeen different Fortune 500 companies during the first half of 2015, I found that only one company CMO was able to bring her most profitable customers to life in a way that enabled me to see them as real people, and to understand how her products were an integral part of her customers' lives. The remaining sixteen? They didn't. All these companies had a tremendous amount of data. They spent millions of dollars doing all kinds of research and analyses. They all had loyalty programs and therefore, had sophisticated segmentation. Most of their work was very left-brain. A number of them described their best customers as "Deciles 8, 9, and 10." Can you imagine describing Decile 10 as if it were a person you had just met? You can't, because Decile 10 is not a person. But the *customer* is, and that's the disconnect, that's the big problem. The Information Economy has everyone lost in so much data that they've gone totally blind to the reality that customers are actually *real people*. If you can describe Decile 10 with a straight face as if it's a human you met at a PTA meeting, my hat is off to you. I surely can't.

This is what I see as the endemic issue with marketers. As we have become besotted with our ability to dissect huge amounts of transactional and behavioral data, we have moved away from the softer side of understanding people to the data side of profiling them. As any neurologist will tell you, when both sides of the brain work together, in a synchronized manner, we draw foresight, intuition, and creativity from the right brain and clear logic, planning, and calculation from the left brain. Similarly, when attempting to understand our customers, we need to understand the whole person. In the prior economies, we began with understanding demographics and then evolved to adding psychographic and lifestyle attributes to get to the real person. Similarly, in the Insight Economy, we need to add personifications to the behavioral attributes to bring the actual, real customer to life.

The irony in all this is that while the marketers are paralyzed by this growing complexity, they've responded by creating more of it. The Insight Economy looms ahead of them like an even more complicated proposition; they balk at becoming decathletes and point to their time and attention starvation as reasons why they just don't have the time to make it work. But here's the thing: It's really simple if we believe that our job as marketers is about fulfilling the real needs of real people in a way that's distinct from our competitors. We've become so disconnected by the data deluge and the complexity of channels that it's been easy to forget that our customers are real people and that they pay real money for real products and services.

I'm advocating that we get back to basics, that we start seeing our customers as people rather than deciles or prospects or lapsed users who all need to be motivated and converted. As David Ogilvy said a long time ago, "The consumer isn't a moron; she is your wife." He was right then, and he is even more right now. Let's not treat our customers badly, let's not talk down to them, and let's not consider them putty to be manipulated. Rather, let's look at each of them as a spouse. I do. My wife is a terrific customer—she's discerning, demanding, fair, and very loyal when her needs are met consistently—and this understanding makes it very easy to make decisions that improve the odds of success in the marketplace. Ogilvy's exhortations from the '60s are true today and will become even truer as we enter deeper into this hyper-fast and hyper-complex economy. Connecting with your best customers on a human level is the solution to all the problems that companies face as they look to turn the corner into the Insight Economy. Finding deep, enduring human truths is the key to that transition. It may seem like a big change, but there are plenty of intuitive, specific examples coming up in the next chapters to show that it is doable. As W. Edward Deming said, "It is not necessary to change. Survival is not mandatory." Your call.

CHAPTER 6

Embracing the Insight Economy

WELCOME TO THIS NEW ERA—the era in which the rules we learned in the past two economic environments will need to be put aside and replaced with better ways to win. The bad news about this transition is that companies unwilling to evolve quickly will be unable to keep pace. But if you're willing to change, then the world will be your oyster. I can promise you that the journey is not very complex, and it is completely within your power.

The path to success in the Insight Economy is a one-way speedway. To do well you've got to *embrace* it; you're here, and there's no way around it. As I said in the last chapter, survival here isn't mandatory; it's up to you to succeed.

Organizations that fully embrace the Insight Economy share traits that I'll point out over the next few chapters while discussing specific examples of companies that are already seeing success in this brave new world.

Let's begin by answering the question. What is the Insight Economy? The idea is very simple. It centers on the idea that organizations must resolve core customer dissonance by solving real problems in a meaningful way—and better than any other brand. By *dissonance*, I mean the difference between what your customers *tell* you and what they actually *do*. There's often a wide gap between the two, and it spans pretty much every category.

From the customer's vantage point, the scientific term for all this is "cognitive dissonance," the discomfort that results when what someone is telling you is different from what your own senses are telling you. If there's a conflict between what a business says it's going to do and what it actually does—as experienced by the customer—the actions will far outweigh the words. "I hear what you say," goes the simple-sounding axiom, "but I believe what you do." There may or may not be something wrong with a customer's hearing; their eyesight tends to be 20/20 in the fabled "moments of truth" when they come nose-to-nose with our brands (physically or virtually) and have an opportunity to confirm or refine their evaluations of our value.

That is the problem marketing has been trying to solve. We thought brands were built by affecting beliefs and by creating relationships. I love Coke. I think Coke is a brilliant brand. It is one of the most beloved brands in the world. Unfortunately, I don't drink Coke. I don't plan to drink Coke and I will never drink it. Who cares? The Coca-Cola Company, that's who. The folks at Coke want me to consume their product. And they have it right. It's not about how people feel about your product or service. It's about what they do with it, how often they do it, and how consistently they do it. That's what builds brands. Now, with the ability to leverage behavioral data with attitudinal research, we can understand this dissonance and find a way to resolve it. Because unless you find a resolution, you can't get to big, category-changing ideas.

To get to insights that resolve dissonance, marketers will need to follow some fundamental rules to guide their transition to this new world. Before we jump into a lot of detail, let me provide a framework.

First, this new environment is going to require new focus. Begin with your most valuable customers. We discussed how the Pareto Principle is alive and well in every company; a small group of customers delivers a majority of the profits. These people should be your single-minded focus, the source of all your ideas and the reason for all your programs.

Why should you start with your customers? Because in developed markets like the U.S., we no longer have what I call *virgin customers*. These experienced customers know what they want and which brand can provide it. Brands that begin with a focus on their core customers have a simple and single-minded approach to solving problems. All their actions gear toward delivering incremental value at each connection point to deepen the relationship while obtaining incremental transactions. This focus on existing customers doesn't mean that they aren't focused on acquiring new customers. They are. But their new customer acquisition is based on offering the same benefits that strengthen their bond with their existing customers. By doing this, they build a stronger, more profitable, and more sustainable business.

Second, brands need a new approach to how they appeal to their customers. I'm sure you're familiar with the traditional marketing's

AIDA (Awareness. Interest. Desire. Action.) model. This model was created in the Attention Economy and further refined in the Information Economy, with a maniacal focus on delivering ROI by measuring the transactions generated by each and every program. Well, that model is ready to be consigned to the rubbish heap. The new model in the Insight Economy is TRL. That stands for Trust, Respect, and Loyalty.

Your customers have to trust you, the brand, to deliver on their needs consistently during each interaction. Your product must perform as it is meant to. If you market a service, it must deliver the outcome the customers desire. Once you've built this trusted relationship, you have an opportunity to earn their respect. Are the brand's values consistent with the values of its customers? Does the brand address customer issues and complaints fairly? Does the brand innovate for its customers? All these questions play a role in transforming the relationship into one of mutual respect.

If your brand is trusted and respected, you will earn the customers' loyalty. But to maintain that loyalty, brands need to work harder than at any of the earlier stages. Don't offer deals to new prospects that are not available to your existing customers. Surprise and delight your core customers. Most important, don't take their loyalty for granted. Loyalty is a two-way street. If you want loyalty, then exhibit loyalty. Brands such as Nike that have the most loyal customers are most loyal *to* their customers. All their innovations—Nike+, FuelBand, etc.—were developed to help existing customers get the most out of their sports and passions.

Third, recognize that this new world demands a new business model. The old model was big new product launches or big advertising campaigns supporting line extensions. This process took months if not years to bring to market. It was capital intensive and time intensive. A successful launch made careers, while unsuccessful launches … well, you know. Today's model is built for speed, effectiveness, and efficiencies. If you're launching new products or services, only introduce ones that are one-tenth the prior era product development cost but can deliver ten times the value. Done right, this has the potential to provide more than a hundred times the impact. If the product or service fails, you can quickly reboot and refine your approach based on what you have learned from your failure. If it succeeds, you continue to develop it as you chase bigger and better results.

Coming off the new model, the next rule is quite intuitive: Don't worry about building companies to last, but build them to evolve. During the Attention Economy, we built products and campaigns to last. Products lasted for decades with minor facelifts. We all remember the new and improved tags on products. Brand campaigns ran for long periods using similar executions and the same tagline. Jim Collins, in his book, *Built to Last: Successful Habits of Visionary Companies,* laid out principles that companies in that era followed to ensure their survival and success over decades. His five core principles received a lot of praise: Build your company around a core ideology; build a cult-like culture; home-grow your management; stimulate progress through BHAGs (Big Hairy Audacious Goals), experimentation, and continuous improvement; and embrace "the genius of the 'and,'" which encourages companies to preserve their core as they stimulate progress.

But that won't work in the new economy. In this era we have to evolve constantly. Standing still means you're going backwards. With technology and data as core platforms for innovation, finding new ways to serve your customers has never been easier—but ironically, it has never been more difficult. Every company has access to the same tools. New companies seem to be sprouting up every second to cannibalize the leaders. The only way to survive is to out-innovate yourself.

The fifth and final rule is to deliver the new equation. Ensure that your brand's values are true to its core and are delivered with authenticity. Customers, especially your most valuable ones, get to know you intimately. They have brought you into their lives. They allow you to solve important problems for them. They expect the brands they choose to have values that are compatible with their own values and beliefs. During the past economies, we saw examples of brands "greenwashing" their products and jumping on any and all sustainability bandwagons to attract what we called *conscientious consumers*. In today's highly transparent ecosystem, this doesn't work. Your customers expect the highest standards from their brands, both in the way they deliver on their promises and in the way they operate in the community. Whole Foods and Trader Joe's have long lived by these principles. But look also at brands like Patagonia and Method, which are emerging as poster children for this rule.

In addition to being conscientious about the environment, your customers also expect you to treat them with integrity and sensitivity.

We talked about building trust, respect, and loyalty earlier in this chapter. These principles need to be evident when the brand interacts with its customers. Remember the story about Bud Light's label fiasco in Chapter Four? Or United's experience with Dave Carroll? Your brand is not an inanimate object. It is defined by the quality of its relationship with your customer: a relationship that encompasses how your customer perceives the present performance and anticipates the future value from your brand.

We will be discussing these five rules in more detail over the next four chapters. As you'll see, it isn't very complicated and it definitely isn't impossible. I hope you want to make it. Getting from here to there is up to you.

INSIDE THE INSIGHT ECONOMY

Talking about this era day in and day out can make me forget that not everyone necessarily understands the terminology I've been using. I was talking with a colleague about the work my firm does to help businesses unearth insights and develop ideas to win in the Insight Economy. He's the CMO of a Fortune 100 company, and like me, he began his career during the Attention Economy, refined his skills during the Information Economy, and is now evolving his skill set to lead in my new economy. I test-drove my rhetoric and the language I have begun to use to describe this new era. I have huge respect for him, and wanted to see if he thought my approach was sound. It was as if I had described Oz.

I took him through the entire proposition: how we began our careers during the Attention Economy, and we learned all the rules and figured out ways to make them work. We embraced the Information Economy (many of us, anyway) and again learned to operate effectively amid the complexity and data deluge. But doing well didn't mean we had mastered all the nuances of the emerging and established technologies or the majority of big data. Because of all the changes and the emergence of new skills and capabilities, a majority of marketers focused so much on all the various trees that they lost the ability to see the forest. We became enamored with the individual genetic iterations of each particular tree, and we became so precise and granular that we forgot why we were truly here. It isn't about bits and bytes—it's about *people!*

Our friends and families. Real, flesh-and-blood people who have specific needs, needs so immediate that they are willing to hand over their hard-earned money to us to have them fulfilled. And it isn't just about monetary exchange, although that's certainly important for the business. There was a fulfilling, personal exchange that could happen in the best of circumstances, too. In the Insight Economy, companies can be rewarded for serving up personalized, experiential transactions. I know that Dunkin' Donuts and McDonald's both serve decent coffee, for instance, but I always, *always* go out of my way to find a Starbucks because it delivers the experiential exchange that I want. And they didn't get there by thinking of people as decontextualized data (although they had their flings with that, too—nobody's perfect). They got there by understanding their customers in a big-picture way, as real humans with real names, real jobs, real homes, real families, and real needs that they fulfill better than anyone else.

REAL TALK ABOUT REAL PEOPLE

Another essential key to success in the Insight Economy is realizing that real people are *not* naïve. They may be from entirely different walks of life, or have different backgrounds, but they're not ignorant of their own needs and desires. Ogilvy's words from the last chapter should still be ringing in your mind: "The consumer isn't a moron; she is your wife." This is particularly true given the context of the world we're living in now—a world where there's so much content available to anyone at any time, a world where "experts" suddenly have much less cachet. A world where everyone can find out everything about anything. Today's consumers are quite savvy about how to evaluate choices and make decisions in this environment. They may be time-starved, just like you and me, but they're also every bit as smart as you and I, if not smarter.

In fact, consumers expect that even if they don't know something, they can figure it out relatively easily. We're trained for that now. I ordered a water fountain for my backyard garden, and when it arrived, I was at a loss for how to put it together—all 480 pounds of it. It came with one typewritten sheet of directions, but it was just a bunch of words on the page—no pictures, no step-by-step instructions, no help. Being a creature of the Insight Economy, though, it was second nature for me to go straight to YouTube, where I typed in the brand name and found a seven-minute "how to" video. Feeling capable, confident, and serene, I set up my new patioscape and then sat down to enjoy it. When I want to learn how to finger-pick a new song on my guitar, I don't worry about finding a competent teacher. I have now become my *own* teacher, with some help from Justin

Sandercoe (via justinguitar.com)—who, as I mentioned earlier in the book, lives in London.

Consumers today are trained to be knowledgeable and resourceful, and above all, they're no longer intimidated by the unknown. Brands that hope to succeed need to understand this and connect with them on a truly personal level.

STANDING OUT IN AN EXPLOSION OF CHOICE

Another hallmark of the Insight Economy is that, while the amount of information available to us has grown exponentially, the choices we have in every aspect of our daily lives have grown just as much. I'd go so far as to call it an *explosion of choice*. It's a terribly exciting time to be around! I'm sure it felt the same to the unicellular organisms that were evolving into multicellular beings (precursors to our forefathers) during the Cambrian Period more than five hundred million years ago.

For many marketers, however, it's a time of terror and trepidation. We know what it can be like as consumers, and CMOs aren't immune to the panic that can result from wanting to cut through the noise. So how *do* we go about breaking through the choice explosion at a time when it seems as if there are as many items on the shelves of a typical supermarket as there are people in an entire city?

The first thing to understand is the universal truth that no matter how much information surrounds us, we only have a finite amount of space in our conscious mind. For argument's sake, looking at it like a computer, let's say that we can keep about 100 megabytes of information running through our conscious mind at any time— maybe about 8 percent of our total computing power. Certainly less than 10 percent, at any rate. The remaining 90 percent or so of the information we are bombarded with takes up space in our unconscious mind. While some may look at these statistics and posit that we've got an infinite amount of space because we have no earthly idea how many "megabytes" the subconscious can hold, I have to say that I completely disagree. As with a hard drive, at some point we have to delete files if we're going to save new ones.

So to deal with this, particularly in a time of choice explosion and information overload, we create shortcuts. We develop expectations and presuppositions, and those impressions start to dig out neural pathways. This is true of simple tasks like riding a bike, which we seem to do almost reflexively once we've learned how; it's also true of identifying and categorizing brand attributes. Brands that have been around and become part of our lives, like McDonald's, for instance, have been carving neural pathways for a very long time; they were a creation of the Attention Economy, after all. To recarve those pathways after such a long time—to ask consumers to think of them differently, or associate McDonald's with anything other than its core value proposition—is akin to trying to change the direction of the Amazon River: You simply can't do it!

But as we've seen over the years, telling someone they can't do something is by no means a surefire way to stop them from doing it. When McDonald's decided to dramatically complicate its menu in an effort to keep up with the incremental brands springing up around it, it fell victim to the dissonance that this behavior created. After so many years of consistently giving people a good product at a good value, it decided to become something else. Unsurprisingly, customers balked. This dissonance is the biggest enemy of brands that try to stand out by betraying their true selves; it causes real damage, and the odds of success are very low—even nonexistent.

This is not new. We saw this in 1985, when Coke launched "New Coke" and then had to pull it. Or when Tropicana lost over 20 percent of its sales after it launched a new package redesign that its customers rejected. Does anyone remember that both the CEO and CMO at Gap lost their jobs after launching a new logo that their customers hated? This is the power your customer has if you try to reroute your brand from the neural rivers you've created.

This is why new, incremental brands have an advantage over brands that grew up in the Attention Economy. These new brands are able to move into new and uncharted territory. From the get-go, they can provide specific, customizable, personal solutions to solve their customers' specific problems. They can be nimble and evolve quickly, largely because the bar is lower for them—or at the very least, more flexible. Five Guys doesn't have to fight the same gorges and canyons in its customers' neural pathways that McDonald's does. Chipotle can offer customizable Mexican because they "invented" the path. Tesla can be the luxury electric car because no others exist yet. That's how these new brands and new entrants begin their conquest in the Insight Economy. And they can do this without causing a very real, very harmful cognitive dissonance among their customers.

TAKE IT FROM ME: ADAMS AND JOS. A. BANK CLOTHIERS

Sometimes a customer will have his or her own dissonance issues to deal with. The wise route to take in this case is for companies to stick to their core propositions rather than chasing those customers down each and every rabbit hole. This was definitely the case with Adams, my preferred brand of golf clubs during my early golfing career, about ten years ago. Adams was the first brand to introduce hybrid clubs—sets of clubs that were easy for newbie golfers to use as they learned the game of golf. But the brand's reputation wasn't just about the role it played for new golfers. It is also considered to be the best game-improvement set of clubs developed specifically for seniors and women. That's why I loved them when I first began playing. Yes, even now, most people think I play like a senior—short but straight. That's me.

It was and continues to be a strong value proposition. And the company has stayed true to it. It appealed to golfers like me who want to play at a higher level but didn't have the flexibility, technique, or swing speed required to play like the pros. I used these clubs for three years, after which my technique had developed enough and I was playing steadily enough that I switched to Pings, and now I love them. Adams seems to have understood this evolution and my decision. Instead of chasing after customers like me who no longer need its technology, Adams continued to stay focused on who "brought them to the party." It continued to produce and market easy-to-hit, easy-to-use clubs, and the company continued to grow consistently, year after year. It stayed relevant to beginners—a huge segment of the market. Adams did fine without me, obviously! It was acquired by TaylorMade-Adidas Golf Company in 2012 for $10.80 per share. As Adidas Group CEO Herbert Hainer said, "This acquisition reflects our commitment to continued growth in the golf category. The proposed combination of Adams Golf Company and TaylorMade-Adidas Golf Company brings together two highly complementary sets of brands, combining Adams' focus on game improvement as well as senior and women golfers with TaylorMade-Adidas Golf Company's focus on the younger and the low- to mid-handicap golfer." A win-win.

Another personal example is Jos. A. Bank Clothiers. I talked about this men's clothing company in *Brand Rituals: How Successful Brands Bond with Customers for Life*. It's been around since 1905, and it's fair to say that, like Adams, its leaders know what they're doing. It's a company whose core proposition is about quality, consistency, and reasonable prices. All its advertising is highly promotional, offering aggressive deals—buy one, get three other suits free, and the like.

Jos. A. Bank doesn't let itself get distracted by the fact that, out in the traditional marketing world, it was seen as a "low-value brand" because of its aggressive, promotional approach. It knows that most critics have a shortsighted view of what it actually offers, which is good quality clothing for men at reasonable prices at convenient locations. It understands that its core and loyal customers (like me) value its core proposition and assess the brand on attributes that have very little to do with its marketing posture. That is why it stays committed to its value proposition and doesn't stray from it—as its competitor Men's Warehouse has in recent years.

I'm glad Jos. A. Bank has stayed true, and I'm also glad I discovered the chain a few years ago, albeit accidentally. Prior to finding them, my routine was a biannual trip to Nordstrom and Macy's. They have a lot of choices (unfortunately, a *lot* of choices) with different cuts and different fits. Shopping isn't fun for me at the best of times. My wife and I would spend an inordinate amount of time at the mall with very little to show for the effort. I stumbled upon Jos. A. Bank when we moved to a new home and I began visiting a different branch of my bank, which coincidently was a couple of doors down from Jos. A. Bank.

One day I decided to walk in, and I was immediately fascinated by the experience. I was greeted by an associate who walked me through the store and got a sense of what I was looking for. Then I found a size (40 S, in case you're curious) that fit me perfectly. It didn't matter whether I was trying on a suit, a sport coat, a shirt, or shoes; whatever it was, it was consistent, so every item worked. I was able to build my wardrobe holistically for the first time. I found *everything and more* while eliminating the unfulfilling shopping trip to the mall. Jos. A. Bank knows what it stands for and for whom it's there. It's able to stand out precisely because it knows this and embraces it.

Here's the reality: If companies and brands want to truly stand out, they need to embrace their core value propositions and stay faithful to them, and they need to do so consistently. Jos. A. Bank has succeeded in business since 1905; Adams since 1991. McDonald's, on the other hand ...

Consistency. It's beautiful in its simplicity—the perfect antidote to the noise of a swiftly shifting marketplace and the explosions of choice. You might remember that magic number that Malcolm Gladwell quotes in *The Tipping Point*: 10,000 hours that stand between anyone and proficiency in a particular trade or craft.

Whether you agree with him or not, the thesis is strong: The more you do the same thing consistently, over and over again, the more effective, the more valuable, and the more impactful you'll become. When your customers know what they can expect from you day after day, visit after visit, you can develop neural pathways that become so entrenched that you won't be pushed out, possibly ever.

Over the past few years we have heard many wonderful stories of companies going from success to struggling to success again. These course-corrections precede brands going back to their basics: McDonald's, as it reframes and refines its menu; Starbucks, as it develops its experience; Apple, as it expands its intuitive technology into wearables. By adhering to core values, each one of these companies has manufactured a renaissance for itself, righting a vessel that had begun to take on water in a sea of distraction. This philosophy is what makes companies scalable, and what makes them bounce back from seemingly catastrophic losses. Remember the panic that set in after Steve Jobs' passing? The succession plan there was airtight; it didn't matter who took over. Like its new CEO, Tim Cook, it seemed like all the associates at Apple were ready, aligned, equipped, and excited to steer Apple toward the North Star. It's very simple. When you're true to yourself, it's that much easier to find your True North.

CHAPTER 7

Who You Are When You Aren't Trying to Be Someone Else

"IT IS NOT the most intellectual of the species that survives; it is not the strongest that survives; but the species that survives is the one that is able best to adapt and adjust to the changing environment in which it finds itself," said Charles Darwin in his theory of biological evolution. This theory states that all species of organisms arise and develop through the natural selection of small, inherited variations that increase the individual's ability to compete, survive, and reproduce. No one is exempt from the necessity of evolution. In order to survive through changing environments—be they corporate or Cretaceous— there *must* be evolution. The critical mistake most companies make isn't allowing this certainty to direct their actions, but forgetting the second part of Darwin's thesis—natural selection.

While Darwin's Theory of Evolution is a relatively young archetype, the evolutionary worldview itself goes back to antiquity. Ancient Greek philosophers such as Anaximander postulated the development of life from non-life and the evolutionary descent of man from animal. Charles Darwin brought something new to the old philosophy—a mechanism called "natural selection." Natural selection acts to preserve and accumulate minor advantageous genetic mutations. Suppose a member of a species developed a functional advantage: It grew wings and learned to fly. Its offspring would inherit that advantage and pass it on to their offspring. The inferior (disadvantaged) members of the same species would gradually die out, leaving only the superior (advantaged) members of the species. Natural selection is the preservation of a functional advantage that enables a species to compete better in the wild. Most companies understand the concept of evolution but fail in their evolutionary approaches because they ignore the principle of natural selection. Companies like Circuit City and McDonald's evolved but did not use their natural advantages. Innovation without that essential core concept to keep a company grounded will eventually fail. Evolution without clear direction and purpose results in extinction.

With this as background, it becomes a bit easier to understand what makes a truly enduring brand. We need only to look to how today's successful brands got here in the first place. At one point in time, each of these brands found a group of consumers who had a need that the brand was able to fulfill in a compelling way. McDonald's provided good, fast food to families on the go. Remember the iconic tagline "Food, Folks, and Fun?" It was able to promote such an image by creating a strong operational model that made it easy for every store to deliver this promise consistently, anywhere and everywhere. By starting each evolution from this core, brands can evolve but still keep their customers satisfied and coming back. McDonald's doesn't need a ton of new items for its menu. What it needs to do is make its core menu items healthier with better ingredients and health-ier sides. That's its natural advantage. The environment will always change, of course, as it has since McDonald's was founded in 1940, but it's only by sticking to this natural advantage can it continue to play a major role in the lives of its consumers. When a company is who it truly is, it works.

BEYOND THE GOLDEN ARCHES: EXAMPLES OF OTHER ENDURING BRANDS (AND A FEW CONFUSED COMPANIES)

The marketplace is full of brands that intuitively understand the value of this principle and have the balance sheets to show for it. Let's talk about one of my favorite household brands, Tide. Introduced in U.S. test markets in 1946 as the world's first heavy-duty detergent, with nationwide distribution accomplished in 1949, Tide claimed it was "America's Washday Favorite." Tide quickly gained market share in the U.S. detergent market, dwarfing the sales of Ivory Snow[3] and accelerating the demise of two of its main competitors, Rinso and Gold Dust Washing Powder, both then Lever Brothers[4] brands. In 2006, the development of Tide was designated an ACS National Historic Chemical Landmark[5] in recognition of its significance as the first heavy-duty synthetic detergent. In a 2009 survey, consumers ranked Tide among the three brands they would be least likely to give up during the Great Recession.[6] This brand has done well for seventy years by using its natural advantages as it evolved. It has changed a

---

3 https://en.wikipedia.org/wiki/Ivory_(soap)
4 https://en.wikipedia.org/wiki/Lever_Brothers
5 http://www.acs.org/content/acs/en/education/whatischemistry/landmarks.html
6 https://en.wikipedia.org/wiki/Great_Recession

lot, from product formulations to packaging and advertising. The one thing it hasn't changed, however, is its core promise: Tide gets your clothes clean.

One of the best experiences that I still draw on from my thirty years in the marketing industry is my time working on the S.C. Johnson business. I handled a number of its brands during my time at Foote, Cone & Belding Chicago. SCJ, as we fondly call it, is a family-owned consumer-products company that markets dominant brands including Raid, Shout, Glade, Pledge®, Ziploc®, and Windex, among many others. These brands continue to be strong for one simple reason: Each brand is built for a core purpose and has delivered consistently for decades. Don't get me wrong—SCJ as a company is very innovative. But each innovation, each product or packaging improvement, comes from leveraging the brands' advantages. With smaller marketing budgets than most of its competitors (Unilever, Reckitt Benckiser, and Procter & Gamble, among others) SCJ brands are leaders in most of the categories in which they compete. The reason? Where a number of other CPG brands spend money marketing new and non-core products, S.C. Johnson's brands spend money and time developing products that build on their natural advantages.

Brands like Raid don't need to spend time, money, and energy reminding consumers who they are when they launch a new product. That's because they aren't moving into comically different categories of expansion; they're just finding new ways to kill more bugs! I told this story in my last book: When we (the agency folks) argued with Bill Perez, then the CEO of SCJ, about increasing advertising budgets so that we could "strengthen the brand," he taught me a fundamental lesson. "We have over 50 percent market share because over half of the shoppers buy our brands. I don't need advertising to strengthen them, I need to continue making better products." That lesson has stayed with me since. Brands are built not on advertising but on great products that continue to deliver on their promises and meet customer needs consistently over time. Advertising and all other marketing is just a way to set the expectation. Let this be a lesson for all marketers: If you have money to spend, spend it on innovations that help strengthen your natural advantages.

But it's easy, particularly for the companies that have embraced the principles of the Information Economy, to get lost in the deluge of data. It sweeps over us, clouding our vision and pushing us farther and farther downstream. Marketers concerned only about the market share they don't currently have look at data that indicates the other potential segments they believe they need to capture. I have seen this behavior in more companies than I would have expected. Take, for example, one of the leading brick-and-click specialty retailers (I can't disclose its identity). It leads its very specific segment, but instead of leveraging its main strength, which is the specificity of its merchandise, it has decided to challenge its online competitive set, made up of seven different e-tailers, to grow its share. I predict that this is one evolutionary tactic destined for extinction.

The same kind of problem is plaguing Walmart. Founded in 1962 by Sam Walton (in my opinion, one of the leading Marketing Decathletes), Walmart has gone on to become not only the world's largest retailer but also one of the world's most admired brands. The company was founded on the core proposition that it would deliver lower prices than its competitors by reducing its profit margins, and this proposition was articulated by the tagline "Always Low Prices. Always." for about two decades. In this period, sales grew from less than $1 million to about $400 billion. In 2008, Walmart changed the "Low Prices" tagline to "Save money. Live better." This was a way to evolve from a rational promise and what the company thought was a transactional relationship to an emotional relationship by delivering a higher-order benefit. Guess what? Walmart's sales went from $401.2 billion for the fiscal 2009 year to $482.2 billion for the fiscal year ending January 31, 2015. This represented a slowdown in growth and a reason for the significant changes that have been made to the leadership of the company over the past year.

How does a very sophisticated company, one that democratized mass merchandising and rode that wave for a good long while, find itself in this position? Traditional thinking. If someone else is doing something better, then I should be doing it, too. Enter Target. Target had to respond to Walmart's success and match its archrival's strategic focus. Robert J. Ulrich (Bob) was as brilliant and single-minded as Sam Walton when he became the president of Target Stores, then a division of Dayton Hudson. He crafted Target's unique brand and marketing image and focus, which is widely considered to be a key contributor to the company's growth and success in its challenge to Walmart.

With fashion and design available at affordable prices, Target developed its own natural advantage as a foundation for its growth. Ulrich realized that there was a need to be met for customers who were still looking for good values—Target isn't Nordstrom, of course—but these customers are a little different from the Walmart customer. They want a retailer that offers them merchandise that is a bit more upscale, a bit more fashion-forward, but which still aligned with the mass-market pricing. This was how Target's tagline "Expect More, Pay Less." came to life.

Along with the catchy tagline, Target stuck to a singular strategy. It serves a market segment by bringing customers something they can't find elsewhere for competitive prices. Everyone loves low prices, especially combined with relatively high-end stuff. Obviously, Walmart wasn't going to attract the "higher-end mass discount customers," but that didn't stop it from trying. This was the reason for the evolution of its positioning from the single-minded and very focused "Low Prices" to a broader and more generic "Save money. Live better."

Walmart did exactly the *opposite* of what it should have done. Instead of doubling down, it walked away from the one thing that was its natural advantage—that low-price platform. In trying to be like Target, it began toying with the other aspect of Darwin's theory, "The inferior (disadvantaged) members of the same species would gradually die out, leaving only the superior (advantaged) members of the species." No wonder it has struggled. Target owns Target's market. By attempting to be like them, Walmart has allowed its advantage to slowly erode, especially among its core and most loyal customers, resulting in not only loss in market share but also a loss in its leadership credentials.

The same problem has beset the auto insurance industry, which over the past couple of decades has become somewhat of a race to the bottom for prices. Insurers, led by GEICO and Progressive, began this race during the Information Economy, in order to challenge monoliths like Allstate and State Farm on price. Their messages were simple and clear: Why pay more for your car insurance? In fifteen minutes or less, you can save 15 percent or more by switching. In an industry beset by unhappy customers and poor service and trust, it was a compelling proposition, and it worked.

To compete, the larger players tried to respond by playing this game and realized that there was no way they could win ... or even survive. Their business model was built around a huge infrastructure with bloated costs. They couldn't really compete on price. Allstate was one of the first companies to realize this and decided to respond by focusing on its strengths. Allstate had a large customer base that liked the personal service provided by the agent network, and this base could be retained if treated fairly. It introduced the Allstate Good Hands Guarantee about four years ago to add value for loyal customers. When Allstate cuts you a check for a good driving record over time, that's promoting loyalty. When it forgives your accident by not raising your rates, that's promoting loyalty. When it focuses on *current* customers rather than chasing after new, price-conscious prospects, it promotes loyalty. This also allows the brand to create compelling stories and compelling connections that no amount of paid media can deliver. Allstate uses its natural advantage. Since then, State Farm has done the same by using its local agent network. Its tagline, "Like a Good Neighbor, State Farm Is There." says it all.

Of course, these brands have had their shaky moments. It is easy to see how businesses were tempted to focus on price, particularly during the Great Recession of 2009. Just as Circuit City let go of its commissioned sales force, Allstate cut its agent network loose while it went down into the mud cutting prices (and cutting into profits). The arrival of Joe Tripodi as CMO in 2003 coincided with a renaissance period at the Illinois-based insurer. According to *Ad Age*, "Arriving at a moment when Allstate was stumbling amid deep-pocketed challenges from upstarts such as GEICO and Progressive, Mr. Tripodi helped stabilize the business by green-lighting a major boost in marketing spending that's paid dividends since."[7] A true believer in deep, abiding customer insights, Joe knew that the key to turning Allstate around (much as he took MasterCard out from under Visa's shadow) was to return the company to its roots. At the 2007 ANA Conference in New York, while still at Allstate, Joe took other marketers to task "for allowing their ads to skew more toward entertainment than a clear consumer-value proposition. He warned them not to be 'seduced by the new thing' in advertising."[8] A true decathlete approach—the return to customer-centric focus and to delivering compelling benefits—helped Allstate come out stronger than ever.

COMMODITIZATION MAKES YOU COMMON; COMMITMENT TO YOUR CORE SETS YOU APART

As the world continues to shift and grow immensely in its complexity, growth is harder to come by. This is the biggest challenge for all CEOs. Their remit is to continue driving the growth of their

---

7 "Coca-Cola Names Joseph Tripodi as CMO." Advertising Age News RSS. July 27, 2007, Assessed August 20, 2015
8 "Politics Are Easy, Commercial Ratings Are Hard." Advertising Age Special Report Upfront07 RSS. March 21,2007. Accessed August 20, 2015.

businesses while improving profitability. They look to their CMOs for distinctive and compelling ideas that will deliver measurable topline growth that they can take to the street. Finding big new ideas and new ways to differentiate brands has become today's biggest unsolved business problem. Or said another way, "failure of new ideas" is the single most articulated reason why marketers struggle to win in today's highly complex global business environment. Each year we launch new products, new campaigns, new services, and new ideas, but we see fewer and fewer of them succeed. If only marketers could find a way to generate ideas that could grow their brands profitably, the assumption is that many of the challenges facing their businesses would disappear.

Guess what? As the people under the gun, most marketers work really hard to deliver. This pressure to find new avenues of growth is itself becoming the problem. As we've discussed earlier in the book, the need for continued growth forces most marketers to look at new avenues. The plethora of data available today exacerbates the problem by indicating a variety of segments and numerous directions that brands can take to find "incremental" growth. Even if they don't feel as if these directions are core to the brand, it becomes an easy sell to CEOs and boards that have financial backgrounds and orientations. I have been in more boardroom discussions than I care to remember where I've seen decisions made to introduce products that made no sense whatsoever. And these decisions were made by experienced, educated, and highly compensated professionals. Remember Circuit City launching DIVX, a competitor to DVDs? How about the Honda ASIMO, a robotic butler from Honda, the company best known for its cars? And as we mentioned earlier, New Coke. There are many such examples.

All these decisions were made with a lot of forethought and significant investments. They were made because business leaders after a time begin to think like the rest of the category. The category paradigm becomes theirs as well. Over time, every category gets commoditized because of the homogeneity of offerings. The urge to perpetuate this homogeneity is further exacerbated by analysts and stockbrokers pressuring the management teams to deliver financial performance. Due to this commoditized amnesia, they begin to believe that the reason for their business to exist is to increase its share value. The reason for the business to exist is to make the shareholders (and the C-Suite) a lot of money. The reason for the business to exist is so that it can pay dividends to keep the markets happy.

Let's stop right here. *The ONLY reason for a business to exist is to serve a customer by fulfilling a specific need for him or her in a way that makes that customer continually and consistently provide the business with their custom.* Peter Drucker said this same thing in his own pithy way: "The purpose of a business is to create a customer." Any business leader who focuses on any activity that endangers this purpose is leaning into Darwin's definition of natural disadvantages, thereby creating an environment of significant potential harm.

It's that simple. More is not more. Less is indeed more. The best way to grow, the best way to gain share, isn't by moving beyond your core value proposition; it is by doing exactly the opposite. In the Insight Economy, the best way to deliver profitable growth is to get back to basics, the way Howard Schultz did during his second stint at Starbucks. Schultz quickly brought Starbucks back to growth by delivering great coffee and a great experience. McDonald's can do this if it recommits to delivering good food at a good value, and Walmart can do it if it delivers the price value that its customers expect.

This is not just strategic mumbo jumbo. This is grounded in a simple consumer truth. Consumers are as time-starved as most CMOs, if not more so. They select brands to fulfill specific needs for them. This is how these brands become part of their lives. Don't make them work too hard by constantly changing what your brand does and what it stands for. Consumers do not want to be confronted with a shifting, changing, byzantine mass of choices. When I want a shower curtain, I don't need to pick from nine hundred thousand options. If I want my Viking refrigerator serviced, I want a Viking service rep. If I want coffee, I always want Starbucks. In the Insight Economy, you will not succeed by trying to be all things to everyone. You will win only if you serve your customers better than they can be served by any other brand for the reason that they picked you in the first place. What is old is new again. During the Attention Economy, this was seen as good strategic discipline. A single-minded brand promise. Staying focused on your positioning. Let's get back to basics. Let's keep it simple.

Consider Apple. Steve Jobs didn't build great products by chasing every segment. "You can't just ask customers what they want and then try to give that to them. By the time you get it built, they'll want something new."[9] He built his products for people who

[9] http://www.inc.com/magazine/19890401/5602.html

want to be different: the artists, the self-styled "crazy ones," and the ones who "think different." Oreo, a brand that predates all the technology of today, took to social media like cookies to milk and were successful because it did so in a way that was soooo Oreo: It put customers at the center of its marketing, and because of this, and despite new channels and platforms, the approach worked. Oreo is still a great cookie—and that's an idea that translates well to any generation.

NIKE: JUST DOING IT WELL

The market *needs* diversity, just as a forest needs biodiversity. When you attempt to become all things to all people, trying to beat every single competitor at its own game on its own turf, you're susceptible to confusion and decline. Coke became bigger when Pepsi came on the scene, not because Coke tried to be like Pepsi—it just made the contrast clearer: what Coke stood for and who its customers were. Duracell grew when Energizer was launched. Walmart and Target both grew while they followed their own distinct approaches. This is the law of duality that was popularized by Al Ries and Jack Trout in their *22 Immutable Laws of Marketing*. The point they make is that in the long run, every market becomes a two-horse race. However, for it to become that, the leading brands need to have distinct positions. They have to stand for different propositions to create the expansiveness needed for category development. If they don't, then the brand that begins to follow the strategic direction of the other will lose. This is what we see as the cause for Walmart's struggles of late.

The one brand that has stayed true to its core proposition from the very beginning has been Nike. It's created a body of meaning surrounding a compelling idea, one that draws in faithful customers year after year. Whether they buy the workout wear or the golf gear, Nike customers become loyalists because they have embraced the Nike ethos: Play hard. Just Do It. It's not just an advertising tagline. It has become Nike's absolute reason for being and the absolute reason for its bonded relationships with customers.

You can see the stability in Nike's DNA by the way that it has handled its entry into the wearables market. As consumer needs have evolved, Nike has seen the need to evolve alongside those needs by developing Nike+ FuelBand, SportWatch, etc. It's developed wearables that track physical activity using apps that connect to different devices to help customers chart progress and gain insight into their physical activities. The jump to tech hardware was certainly a leap away from shoes and other sportswear, but it was one that made sense.

What made even *more* sense, however, was Nike's decision to hand over the production of the hardware and software to Apple via a strategic partnership. Nike realized that it has the sports know-how, whereas Apple knows how to develop easy-to-use technology. This is in direct contrast to a company like Uber that is growing heads like a hydra as it tries to build on a foundation that's not even dry. As with an actual construction project, you can see cracks starting to form in this foundation; no builder worth his salt would rush that part of the process. Uber has only recently had its public valuation as an on-call taxi and limo service, but now it's branching out into a delivery service. It's testing delivery of ice cream and barbecue to customers through its app. This is happening even before Uber has solved all its public-image problems, and definitely before it has maximized its potential with its core business. Nike clearly doesn't want to be all things to all people, and that's why it is successful.

SLOW DOWN, SIMPLIFY, AND SUCCEED: THE ZEN OF BUSINESS (AND GOLF)

So we know what *not* to do. We know not to try to be all things to all people. We know that more isn't the way to get more; *less* is. We know these things, but it still seems counterintuitive; there's a dissonance. Golf fans know that there's a certain Zen to the art of golf. When you're playing golf, the world operates very counterintuitively. This is what I've learned: If I want my ball to fly farther, I actually have to swing slower. If I want a swing that delivers strong compression, I have to shorten my backswing rather than lengthen it, rein in my power rather than let it rip. The more relaxed my grip, the better the outcome, and the more power and control I actually gain.

It's the same thing in business and in marketing: The best way to drive growth is to stop forcing growth. When I say this to some of my clients, they look at me as if I've lost my mind. As you can imagine, I've fielded my fair share of strange looks. It doesn't bother me anymore—I've spent much of my career helping clients grow their businesses profitably by pruning dead branches and getting rid of the weeds so that we can nurture the core value proposition and create an unbridled environment for growth.

CHAPTER 8

Stop Marketing to People Who Aren't Your Customers (and Who Never Will Be)

IT TAKES A *lot* of work to achieve the brand recognition of a Nike, a McDonald's, or a Walmart. Decades and decades of focus and spending. So it's always a bit surprising to me when I see a brand changing course (in a number of cases, dramatically) by trying to launch a new product or a new positioning, or trying to attract a new group of customers. Because, as we discussed in the last chapter, moving away from the brand's core, its natural advantage, leads to the kind of outcome that has a high likelihood of causing the boat to capsize.

CASE STUDY IN DISSONANCE AND DOWNFALL: SEARS

The recent downturn in the fortunes of Sears, one of America's most iconic brands, empathically illustrates this point. Sears is as iconic as a brand can get. The company was founded by Richard Warren Sears and Alvah Curtis Roebuck in 1886. The first Sears catalog was published in 1888. Before the Sears catalog, farmers typically bought supplies (often at high prices and on credit) from local general stores with narrow selections of goods. Prices were negotiated and depended on the storekeeper's estimation of a customer's creditworthiness. Sears took advantage of this by publishing catalogs offering customers a wider selection of products at clearly stated prices. The business grew quickly. For an entire century, Sears mirrored the growth of the economy to become one of the largest retailers in the world. The 1990 fiscal year was the first time Sears lost its leadership position and fell to #3 behind Walmart and Kmart. Since then, it has been in a free-fall. Its revenue has declined by over 27 percent, over $10 billion, in just the past four years. How is it that the company that created commerce in this country, serving the American middle class whether they lived in the middle of a city or in the middle of nowhere, a company that even sold plans for houses, came to this situation?

As the Attention Economy began to develop, the market began to fragment, and we transitioned to a business environment in which different brands developed to serve different demographic segments at different price points: Kohl's, JCPenney, and Macy's are some examples. The idea of one monolithic enterprise serving the entire middle class became impossible, resulting in a splintered marketplace.

Fast-forward to another decade, November 2004: Kmart merged with Sears to create Sears Holdings, the third-largest retail company in the U.S. This deal was fashioned by Edward Lampert, an owner of a hedge fund, who came in as chairman—and four years and four CEOs later became the CEO as well. Since the takeover, Sears Holdings' sales have dropped from $49.1 billion to $39.9 billion, and its stock has sunk 64 percent. A number of people hold Lampert accountable for this deterioration. I think they're right. He has made so many moves that are head scratchers, such as turning one retail company into forty warring conglomerates with their own boards, CEOs, and CMOs, and resorting to financial engineering instead of basic business execution. However, his biggest mistake has been—and unfortunately continues to be—not understanding his core customers.

Sears' biggest problem was that the middle class it served had changed as cities and towns evolved. Sears eventually found its stores in areas where the middle class looked very different. These folks spoke Spanish, Hindi, and Mandarin more than they spoke English. They still came to Sears because that was where they found world-class brands like Kenmore, Craftsman, and DieHard, as well as other merchandise that fit their needs. This new middle class embraced technology but still shopped the brick-and-mortar locations first. Lampert didn't understand this, and neither did the marketers or the business owners.

Sears decided to stop investing in its stores: Per *Bloomberg Businessweek*, it spent $1.51 per square foot in capital expenditure, versus $10.12 by Walmart, $9.36 by Target, and $6.25 by Macy's.[10] While starving the stores, Lampert encouraged significant spending on online and digital activities. As Mika Kasumov, who worked as a senior analyst on the digital side and left Sears to work for eBay said about the focus on online activities, "One, there's a lot of attention from Eddie. Two, you have a lot of money to spend."[11] This focus on trying to create a social community around a digitally led

[10] http://www.bloomberg.com/bw/magazine/content/10_14/b4172040528906.htm
[11] http://www.bloomberg.com/bw/articles/2013-07-11/
at-sears-eddie-lamperts-warring-divisions-model-adds-to-the-troubles#p4

concept called "Shop Your Way" became a huge priority for Lampert and therefore, the company. As a number of former executives said in interviews with *Bloomberg*, "He (Lampert) shops almost exclusively online."[12] Lampert made the absolute, classic mistake. He built marketing and technology programs for people who weren't his customers and never would be. Instead of embracing the new middle-class customers and improving their shopping experience by refreshing the stores and improving the merchandise, he focused all of the company's activities on trying to build what he described as a future-oriented "integrated retail" business. Meanwhile, the business continues to lose billions of dollars and bleeds cash.

CASE STUDY IN RETURNING TO ROOTS: VOLVO

A new management team, or a new era, doesn't always mean the end of a brand's glory days. Stumbling blocks are as inevitable as the change that causes them. It's just a matter of sticking to your core and turning things around. Like Sears, the automotive company Volvo had a reputation that it had spent years building. In the Attention Economy, the name Volvo made for itself was spelled S-A-F-E-T-Y. Volvos were known as the safest cars out there, and it was on that reputation that Volvo was able to build its brand.

Like Sears, Volvo has a long and prestigious history. The Volvo Group originated in 1927, when the first Volvo car rolled off the production line at the factory in Gothenburg, Sweden. After a slowdown in growth during the 1990s, Volvo sold its car division to

---

12 http://www.bloomberg.com/bw/articles/2013-07-11/
at-sears-eddie-lamperts-warring-divisions-model-adds-to-the-troubles#p4

Ford Motor Company for $6.45 billion in 2000, where it was placed within the Premier Automotive Group alongside Jaguar, Land Rover, and Aston Martin. Ford planned to use Volvo engineering resources and components in various Ford, Land Rover, and Aston Martin products, with the second-generation Land Rover Freelander designed on the same platform as the second-generation Volvo S80. The Volvo T5 gasoline engine was used in the Ford Focus ST and RS performance models. This was the beginning of the end. Ford not only cannibalized Volvo technology but decided to build more performance-driven models, eschewing the carmaker's safety heritage.

As with the engineering, the advertising changed to reflect the new direction. So eventually, the *story* that Volvo started to tell was aimed at this different market. It lost its connection with its original customer base, and at the same time, it failed to resonate with its intended one, Volvo wasn't known as a performance brand, so no amount of persuasion could convince a performance-conscious customer to choose a Volvo over a BMW. Just ask my son, who decided that he would retain my ten-year-old BMW 328 rather than switch to a Volvo. "Dad, it's not cool!" Enough said. This is why Ford sold Volvo in 2010 to Zhejiang Geely Holding Group of China for $1.8 billion, booking a loss of $4.7 billion to what it paid less than a decade earlier. There was a lot of grumbling during the sale. Would the Chinese help or hurt Volvo?

Guess what? The Geely guys actually got it. They definitely have shown themselves to be smarter than Lampert and his team at Sears. They knew that to regain relevance, they'd have to return the Volvo brand to its roots—by again building the safest cars in the world. First, they invested $11 billion to put "some Swedish sensibility back" into Volvo. They felt that their rivals had left an opening because they focused too much on horsepower and leather seats and too little on how customers drove, loaded their kids into the car, and used technology. "We believe we can be a clever alternative, and people want an alternative," said Alain Visser, senior vice president for marketing, sales, and customer service at Volvo, in an interview with Bloomberg.[13] "The more customer-centric approach is inherently Swedish," he said, and the new SUV will reflect that. Instead of dozens of buttons, it will have only eight spread between the steering wheel and the center of the dashboard, where a large flat-screen display sits. The new hybrid engine will provide a lot of acceleration yet use relatively little gas while cruising. The car will even have what Volvo calls "Swedish air," a system that closes external ducts when it detects outside pollution.

In May 2014, the average U.S. price for a Volvo was $41,000, much less expensive than a BMW ($52,757) or a Mercedes ($61,000). "I'm not sure they're attracting the entry-luxury buyer," says Kevin Tynan, senior auto analyst with Bloomberg Industries. "It's sort of that safety, technology buyer."

That "safety, technology buyer" is the "Volvo buyer." Kudos to Geely and Volvo. They learned from Ford's errors. They stopped going after their competitors' customers and decided to better serve their own with better technology and better products. And to top

---

13 "Volvo Seeks U.S. Sales Revival With Return to Swedish Roots." Bloomberg.com. June 26, 2014. Accessed July 25, 2015.

it all off, they now spend *less* than ever before on marketing, particularly less than they did during the blip when Volvo was trying to become a performance company. What may initially seem counterintuitive is anything but; when you stick to the proposition and the message that your customers are already familiar with, they don't have to be reminded. You have mind share, which, as we all know, translates into market share.

And this is how real growth happens. Growth doesn't happen by chasing after people who will never be your customers—no performance drivers for Volvo, no upper-crust shoppers for Sears. Growth happens when you cut out dead weight, focus on your core, and look at the people who are already giving you their custom, day after day and week after week. *These* people are likely to be your supporters and advocates. Instead of taking them for granted and looking at their business as a given, double-down your focus on them. If you don't, you will succumb to *target envy*, which is what Walmart did when it went down the rabbit hole of Target envy. The pun here is more than wordplay, it's important: If you're chasing after someone else's target customers, you're ignoring your own. That's not the approach that generates growth. Real growth comes from the customers you already have—not the prospects you wish to have.

EMPATHY, LOYALTY, AND OTHER CASUALTIES OF THE DISTRACTED BRAND

When your brand gets distracted trying to build impossible, almost imaginary relationships with consumers you'll *never* acquire, you stand to lose more than short-term profits. What is at stake for you is something far more meaningful for the brands that get it right—and far more damaging for the brands that get it wrong. We've talked about it with the telecommunications industry, and we've certainly talked about it with McDonald's. You probably even have experience with this in your own life just on a personal level—that icky feeling you get when you're talking to someone and you realize that, instead of listening to what you're saying and being fully present with you, he's looking slightly over your shoulder for a better prospect.

Brands that look to promotions and sales tactics to try to entice new consumers inevitably erode the patience and respect of their most valuable and profitable customers. Those customers are not stupid. They are sensitive, they are smart, and they are in tune with how they are treated by brands to which they've given their loyalty. And the great irony of the whole situation is that as they attempt to woo away competing brands' loyalists without protecting their own, they only lose the loyalty of their most important and most profitable customers.

This is painfully obvious to me with the airline industry. The good carriers have figured out that at the end of the day, their best customers are the customers they need to focus on. They may not drive a majority of the revenue, but they drive almost all of the profit. They are the ones paying higher ticket prices, premiums for travel perks, and so on. They're not driven by price; because they travel so much, they want a good travel experience, which is the only reason for their "loyalty" to a specific airline.

So you would think that if some airlines have figured this out, they'd all get on the bandwagon of treating their best customers better, right? Wrong. As airlines try to find ways to cut expenses and improve profitability, they begin to drain the pool of their premier-status fliers. Benefits are seen as an expense, so they're getting slashed. I have experienced this personally with United Airlines. The way this story unfolded really stuck with me, especially because I have been such a loyal flier and an advocate of United over the past decade.

I wish I could tell you that I became a top-tier customer for United because I'm a jet-setter. The reality is a bit more mundane. For the past two decades, I have been traveling globally on business for more than 250 days a year. So for me, it's particularly important that my travel experience provides the comfort and convenience that I need to keep working as I bounce from one city to another. Over the years with United, I'd come to expect a certain level of service—it's why I was loyal. So imagine my disappointment when United began to make changes and cut corners for short-sighted, tactical reasons.

I'll give you an example. Even though I'd flown a lot over the past decade (more than 250,000 miles per year), I didn't fly as much last year for personal reasons. So United dropped me from Global Services, its invitation-only, topmost tier, to its next tier, Premier Executive 1K. Just because I was a less active customer in the previous calendar year, I quickly went—without so much as a note—from invitation-only status to a customer class comprising people who spend a fraction of what I spend on travel. The experience gave me a pretty eye-opening perspective on just how poorly United Airlines treats its Premier (non-Global Services) customers. Now I board with all Group 1 customers, despite buying full-fare first-class tickets. And it's the same in long security lines. The other levels don't have any prestige or value. They've become one more buzzword.

The other dimension of this experience was that I felt no loyalty or empathy from United. Remember, loyalty is not based on transactions but rather on relational experiences. Unfortunately, these qualities seem to have become casualties in the distraction of the United-Continental merger. It feels as if the management team has gotten so bogged down in trying to integrate two large, complex operations while trying to make money for the Street that it is willing to offer more perks (early boarding, premium seating, etc.) to consumers who sign up for its credit cards from Chase than to the loyal customers who actually deliver most of its profits. United has lost the human component of its interaction with the customers *it does* have. It no longer seems to understand, empathize with, or even have a clear idea of who its customers are as people. Human connection is impossible when you think of your customers as deciles. You can't interact with deciles in the way that you can interact with a real person—me, for example. A real customer is Zain—a fifty-one-year-old almost-empty-nester; idiosyncratic, opinionated, but still loyal. Zain.

And I don't just feel this way as a United customer; I can see it from the marketers' point of view as well. As I mentioned earlier, in the past five months, I've only had one CMO out of seventeen who was able to clearly describe her most valuable customers to me in a way that enabled me to see, feel, and get to know them. Only *one* CMO! Sixteen others were able to define demographics and other data dimensions, like deciles, but were unable to bring their customers to life.

I could clearly see that to United, I wasn't a person. Instead, I was a number that fell from one decile to the next lower one: the decile where the company couldn't afford to spend as much on me. To be honest, the cutbacks didn't inconvenience me much, as I still travel in premium cabins, but they stung in a fundamental, human way. People are complex beings, capable of incredible bonds and loyalty—to friends, family, or even brands. So when brands, much like friends or family, fail to evince the kind of empathy and loyalty that would truly indicate a trustworthy relationship, people notice. I definitely noticed.

On the flip side, American Airlines, with whom I had also flown quite a bit over the past couple of decades, actually reached out to me. While United responded to my year of downtime by unceremoniously dropping me to a lower tier, American responded with a call from a customer service rep at its Dallas headquarters. "We haven't seen you on any of our planes this year, Mr. Raj," the rep said. "Is everything all right?"

Everything was all right, of course; my personal priorities and schedule had just not allowed for much travel. But I was thrilled to be asked, to be identified as a human being and to be understood. I thanked the rep for calling, and shared with him the reasons why I hadn't been flying, explaining that I would definitely be back in the air beginning in the later part of the year. "We understand, and we look forward to having you back on our planes when you get back to traveling," he said.

Not only did I experience empathy and understanding from that gentleman, and by extension, American Airlines, the way the airline followed up was so completely different from United's approach that it won my loyalty. It grandfathered my premier status through the following year, despite the fact that I had not been on a single one of its planes. By contrast, I *had* flown on United, just not as much—and I'd gotten dropped for my trouble.

As if that weren't bad enough, during the time I was accumulating those flight credits, I noticed the service level on the flights dipping further and further. On one flight, I received an already-opened container of jam with my breakfast. On another, a flight attendant completely forgot to hand me my jacket after a long flight back from London, so I had to wait until the plane emptied and then had to go back in and fetch it myself. These weren't huge problems, but they were problems that should absolutely warrant an apology, in human terms. I didn't get any. It is now painfully evident that United no longer sees its customers as humans—they're a data point in some decile on some analyst's chart. However, as a human, I've gone and given a lot of my business to American, Delta, and Virgin. Surprisingly, Delta and Virgin, with whom I have almost no status, treat me and other fliers better than I was treated by United even as a Global Services customer.

The bottom line is that loyalty isn't a marketing program or a tactic; it has to be part of the brand's authentic values. And when it's *not* treated as such, it becomes very obvious to your customers, especially your most loyal ones. If service is subpar, they feel taken for granted, they don't feel understood, and they definitely don't feel valued. True loyalty isn't dropping customers as soon as you've got your hooks into them—true loyalty is sticking with them at all times. You can't expect loyalty from your customers if you're unwilling to be loyal back. Loyalty needs to be a two-way contract. This problem is not just in the airline industry, of course, although they're some of my (least) favorite culprits. You can see it in the way wireless services providers treat their customers. Or how certain retailers treat you if you forget the coupons they sent you in the mail, even though they could easily look up the offers by using your phone number or address. Costco gets it right: It extends loyalty discounts automatically as a matter of course. It isn't as concerned with blasting potential new members with coupon mailings; it's interested in increasing the spending from the loyal customers it already has in the system. By missing the potential that exists *within* your own customer base and expending valuable resources going after prospects who don't share the same values, you're setting up your brand and business for a lose-lose proposition. You'll lose your core customers and you'll lose your profits. Not a good outcome, is it?

CHAPTER 9

Living the Promise:
What Brands Must Stand for Today

ARE BRANDS DEAD? Do we need them anymore?

That's the big question that everyone is debating these days. Not just these days, actually—it seems as if we've been talking about it for some time now. I remember the discussion going back throughout my thirty years in the business. Even during the Attention Economy, when we were "building" brands, the industry and practitioners were always divided on the need for brands, the role of brands, and the definition of brands. Did the company own the brand or was the brand only a brand if the customer deemed it to be? Is a brand built on an emotional relationship or is it based on a transactional one? What is a brand worth? Is the goodwill associated with brands something that attaches to balance sheets? Do leadership brands provide advantages in changing environments, or do the legacies of these brands become the sword of Damocles? The world continues to change and evolve—the world of the consumer, the world of companies, and the world of technology. So why not the world of brands?

By now, you know how I feel about change. I love change. I embrace change. Change is great. You can either see change as an inhibitor or you can allow it to propel you forward. It doesn't matter how you see it; there's really no stopping it. To make sense of this change, and to get an idea of what brands will need to do to remain relevant and successful in the Insight Economy, we've got to go back to the beginning.

THE HISTORY OF BRANDS

Long before we looked to brands to help us make decisions about what kind of cereal to buy, brands occupied an important place in our lives. The word *brand* derives from the Old Norse *brandr* meaning "to burn," based on the practice of producers burning their mark (or brand) onto their products. The oldest generic brand in continuous use in India since the Vedic period (ca. 1500 BCE–500 BCE), is the herbal paste known as *Chyawanprash*, consumed for its purported health benefits and attributed to a revered *rishi* (or seer) named Chyawan. This product was developed at Dhosi Hill, an extinct volcano in northern India.

The roots of branding—defined loosely as using symbols to represent products—can be traced to ancient times. Merchants in Egypt, China, Greece, and Rome used pictures and symbols to communicate with customers who could not read. Shop signs displaying shoes, eyeglasses, or other tangible products conveyed information about the merchandise available in those stores. Back then, brands were important for the same reasons they are important today: A brand helps set the buyer's expectations of quality, performance, and cost.

So the job of a brand was—and still is—to set an expectation of what the consumer can expect from it, and to deliver on these expectations consistently and sustainably. This is how brands can stand out in crowded market segments. When I look at grocery store shelves stocked with bottled water, I can easily name ten different brands—all offering the same product, essentially. But when it comes time for me to choose the one for me, I go with the one that gives me absolute confidence that when I drink it, I'll be drinking purified, safe water, bottled in a place I trust, in a way I trust, by a company I trust. That's why I patronize Starbucks over all the other options I have available to me: Because while I can get coffee anywhere, even a gas station in the middle of nowhere, I know that at a Starbucks, I will have the experience I expect; I can get the coffee I want and make it the way I want (Venti Pike, double-cupped, with three brown sugars and some half-and-half). When I walk into any Starbucks, whether it's in London or in San Francisco or in Naperville, I know I will have a very consistent experience.

More recently than hieroglyphic etchings in the history of brands is Rosser Reeves' theory of the **unique selling proposition**, or USP. Reeves, one of my original gurus, wrote of this key concept in 1961 when he penned *Reality in Advertising*. It's a simple idea, but it was revolutionary in its time—and marketers still point to it today when discussing strategy.

In his concise little book, Reeves laid out the key to building recognizable and successful brands. He articulated three simple yet profound principles. First, customers should understand the specific benefit they get when they buy your product; second, that benefit must be unique, such that the competition either cannot or does not offer it; and finally, the benefit has to be strong enough to motivate people to action. It's not good enough to *say* that the benefit will really help the customer; it has to be predictable and proven. Pretty crystal clear, right?

In the Attention Economy, the big brands were quick on the uptake with this idea, and it worked for them. Crest, for example, had the USP that it was backed by the American Dental Association, which confirmed that the product helped fight cavities. It promised consumers that if they brushed regularly with Crest, they'd enjoy healthier teeth. It was simple, it was clear, and it made sense to consumers. This USP motivated millions of Americans to buy Crest, allowing it to overtake Colgate and become the market leader in oral care.

During this era, we saw the introduction of a lot of new products and new brands. This was also the time for classic mass marketing. We were a growing, fairly homogenous population. But as demographics and realities changed, and we moved into the Information Economy, the idea of the USP needed to evolve as well. In the '70s, Al Ries and Jack Trout spearheaded that evolution when they wrote *Positioning: The Battle for Your Mind*, which moved the USP to its next stage. Ries and Trout defined a very rational approach to the creation of a brand through positioning, saying that a brand needed to have a distinctive position in the mind of the customer. So in the automotive industry, for example, brands took up distinctive positions; BMW became known for performance; Mercedes, for luxury—and as we discussed earlier, Volvo, for safety. In the laundry detergent arena, Tide *owns* clean. Despite the introduction of more than forty new competitors in the past four decades, Tide continues to be a leader.

Ries and Trout talked about "little ladders" in consumers' minds. The concept of positioning meant that each brand had to have its own rung. If a rung was already taken, you had to find another position to occupy. During the Information Economy, the utilization of the positioning concept and the USP concept resulted in a proliferation of brands, and from there on out, those once-brilliant ideas started to become less effective. Brands took the ideas of positioning and USP and frantically created iterations of products that were all essentially the same once you took a close look at the ingredients. Where there were once a few choices, there was now a tidal wave smacking consumers in the face as they turned down each aisle. With more than 20,000 SKUs in an average store, it became impossible for brands to stand out. To cope with this proliferation, brands increased their shelf presence by breaking out of their categories into subcategories. Crest moved from being a leader in cavity protection to providing products for whitening and treating sensitive teeth, as well as toothbrushes, mouthwashes, etc.

When you add in the overcapacity for cheap and easy manufacturing that happened during this time period thanks to wonderful advances in technology, you ended up in the middle of a perfect storm. We've already talked about how in the Attention Economy it took years to launch a new ad campaign, let alone a new product. But in the Information Economy, with the democratization of technology, even if you weren't the first one to cross the finish line of product development, you could be a close second. Hence, an entire aisle of toothpastes to choose from. And that's just in a physical store. Add the choices on the Web, and this proliferation increases by an order of magnitude. You can shop from 43,991 listings for toothpaste on Amazon today. That's more than twice the number of total SKUs in my neighborhood Jewel Osco.

But the problem is that even if a consumer wanted to pay attention to each and every brand on the shelves, it's impossible. We don't have the space in our heads to keep adding more and more brands, and we don't have the time to research each new iteration. And realistically, we don't want to. There aren't any more virgin consumers out there. Every consumer in the U.S. has experienced almost every category. And with information now only a click away, they are more educated, more cynical, and much more discerning. A product that would have launched with huge fanfare in past economic eras doesn't really make as big of a media splash today. Consumers are in the know, in some cases, even before some new products begin their manufacture. And with the democratization of value and distribution, almost anyone willing to shell out the money can get access to the latest and greatest products.

Consider the Apple Watch. On the day these watches became available, a number of people had them. Not just wealthy, upscale folks; regular people—loyal Apple customers who stood in line for twenty-four hours or more to get their hands on the first set of watches. Mine arrived a couple of weeks later in the mail. By this time, the "ooh-and-aah moments" had already passed. Some of my friends who didn't even have the watch knew more about its functionality than I did after using it for a month. Democratized information does this. In this case, it took away my ability to enjoy my cool, new product. It just goes to show that there's nothing you can't get, or at least that you can't aspire to get.

We've reached a stage at which past models like USPs and positioning aren't really working. Consumers no longer have the bandwidth to connect all the dots, and no room left in their hearts and minds to fit all the product and brand options out there.

So what's a brand to do?

THE VALUE OF VALUES

In order to thrive in the Insight Economy, a brand must have a clear set of values. That's the very simple answer.

This economic era is being propelled by the new group of consumers we call *millennials.* Authors William Strauss and Neil Howe wrote about the millennials in *Generations: The History of America's Future, 1584 to 2069,* and they released an entire book devoted to them, titled *Millennials Rising: The Next Great Generation.* Strauss and Howe are "widely credited with naming the millennials," according to journalist Bruce Horovitz. They coined the term in 1987, "around the time 1982-born children were entering preschool and the media were first identifying their prospective link to the millennial year 2000."[14]

Strauss and Howe believe that each generation has common characteristics that give it a specific character, with four basic generational archetypes repeating in a cycle. According to their theory, millennials will become more like the "civic-minded"

14 "After Gen X, Millennials, what should next generation be?". *USA Today.* November 24, 2012. Accessed July 25, 2015.

G.I. Generation, with a strong sense of community, both local and global. In a number of other studies, we clearly see that millennials can be defined both by their strongly held values and their strong intention to live by them. They are passionate about making a difference in the world. This is not just an intellectual argument; I see this in my discussions with my son, who will be a junior in college. These values are not skin-deep; they are fundamental to his vision of his role on this planet.

Given how important values are to your brand's customers, it is very important for marketers to understand how to align with them. How do you do this? First, find a core and valuable role to play in your customers' lives. You can do this by solving a real problem in a way that is distinctive and compelling. And as we've said before, you need to deliver on this consistently. If you do this well, your customer will to come to trust you. Your product has performed as it was meant to. Your service delivered the outcome you promised. Once you've built this trusted relationship, you have an opportunity to earn their respect. This is based on the alignment of the brand's values with the values of your customers.

The thing about values: They are not marketing messages. They're not slogans and buzzwords. Values are important. They represent lasting beliefs or ideals shared by the members of a culture about what is good or bad and desirable or undesirable. Values need to be authentic and ingrained in your company. This means every single person in your company should understand your values and live them, from the C-Suite to the cubicles to the factory floor. You will have to acknowledge that, yes, there are going to be other brands out there that can solve the same problem. But your brand will be distinctive, and your values will keep your customers. Because they share these values, they will eschew other brands, and even better price offerings, in order to stay loyal.

As we've said, two things must be clear. First, what *value* does the brand deliver? And second, what *values* does the brand embrace?

The first question is the more pragmatic one. Customers buy products first for *actionable* outcomes, and they stay for *emotional* reasons. So a brand must first set a clear expectation about how it fulfills the customers' needs in a distinctive and compelling way. Nike is one brand that has done this perfectly from the get-go. First, it set a clear expectation for its customers: "We are the brand that will allow you to do whatever you need to do in an athletic way. We'll allow you to play whatever sports, whatever physical activities, whatever leisure activities you want. We'll provide you with the tools and products and services that will allow you to do this at the highest level possible. *Just do it.*" This is how Nike states its mission on its website: "Bring inspiration and innovation to every athlete in the world."[15] And I like its qualification to the word *athlete*: "If you have a body, you are an athlete." That includes desk jockeys like me.

That's a pretty powerful promise! If you unpack it, you can clearly see not just the value that Nike provides, but also the values that it lives and breathes. Nike believes that everyone has an inner athlete, and Nike sees its purpose as bringing inspiration and innovation to all—even those, like me, who aren't particularly athletic. It tells all of us that whatever kind of athlete you are, whatever you want

---

[15] http://help-en-us.nike.com/app/answers/detail/a_id/113/~/nike-mission-statement

to be, just go for it. Just do it. We'll be there for you. And Nike has stayed consistent with that promise from day one, telling stories that inspire individual performance, pulling together disparate communities, and building lifelong loyalties even as its product lines evolve.

Gatorade lives the same way in the same space (athletic performance), and it has done similarly well. Throughout the years, Gatorade has stayed true to its mission of supporting athletes. Whether those athletes are in junior high school, high school, or college; whether they are professional or aspiring athletes or just weekend warriors, Gatorade provides thirst-quenching, performance-enabling refreshment to all comers. "We're there for you,"[16] it tells this disparate group of athletes. "Go work out hard. Our products will give you the ability to perform at your best."

All Gatorade products—from energy chews to classic sports drinks—are aligned with those promises that it has made to consumers. But it's not just the products that are in alignment; it's the values, too. All of Gatorade's activities are focused on supporting athletes in various communities. It sponsors athletes in the Olympic games, the Special Olympics, community events, and on down the line. It has a very well-focused line of products that deliver great, *rational* value, all the while tapping into that emotional component of a value system.

Neither Gatorade nor Nike really has to talk about how its drink or shoe is better than the competition's drink or shoe. There's not much room for that conversation, even if they wanted to have it. Instead, both brands talk about *why* they are there: to inspire you

---

[16] https://www.youtube.com/watch?v=zwiOr14Alj8

to reach to whatever aspirations you hold dear. And they *deliver* on those promises.

In order to stay relevant, brands need to connect the dots between what they say and what they do. Just as there is a glut of products in any given category, there's a tsunami of advertising and social media campaigns with which brands attempt to create emotional connections. Because we're living in a world where there are no more virgin consumers, it's fairly easy for people to see through empty promises. And when they do, today's technology and communications make it just as easy to spread news of those failures. When United lost Dave Carroll's guitar, the skies didn't look so friendly. And unlike previous eras in consumption, the feedback is instantaneous. Dave Carroll wrote a strongly worded letter, slapped a stamp on it, and waited for it to get shuffled around a customer service center. He dialed the 800 number and was put on hold for hours. That's why he took matters into his own hands and used the Internet, the world's media channel, and made United's life miserable. In today's world, if you say one thing and turn around and do something else, there's nowhere to hide. We live in an increasingly transparent world, like it or not.

Now, when a situation like this develops, you can handle it poorly, as United did, or you can handle it with aplomb. As you know, I'm a Starbucks fanatic, but for some reason before a recent conference I was unable to locate the nearest Starbucks and had to settle for Caribou Coffee instead. I won't mince words here: I hated it. It's not even that it wasn't Starbucks; it wasn't hot, and it just wasn't good. In the middle of my speech, to illustrate a point as much as anything else, I tweeted about my experiment to Caribou. "Just bought a large. Wasn't hot. Tasted awful," went the frank message.

A little bit later, my phone buzzed with a notification from Twitter. It was Caribou, sending me its apologies and a coupon for two free cups of coffee to make it up to me. *There's* a brand that gets it. There are a number of brands out there in today's economy that truly understand that values are about more than lip service. Values are about making the commitment to solve real consumer problems and *then delivering on that commitment.* It's easy, now that we all have social media presence, to shoot off promises and witty claims. But to be successful as a brand, you need to be able to put your money where your mouth is.

All the good brands get this. Apple tells you to "Think different," and it gives you the tools to bring your creativity to life. So it's easy to recognize an Apple product, since everything—from conception of design to execution of the product to advertising and even the in-store experience—is built around the singular value system that Steve Jobs and Apple constructed. That value system is so strong that it's mostly survived the death of its creator, and it continues to live with new products like the Apple Watch and new services like Apple Music.

You don't have to have a complicated product to achieve this kind of loyalty, either. On the opposite end of the engineering spectrum, you've got another classic brand, Lego. It reenergized its brand by identifying its core value—the tactile way in which its product inspires young children to create and build things. By refocusing its energies on its core value system, and delivering on those promises, Lego has been able to revitalize the brand. The toymaker has enjoyed ten years of spectacular growth, almost quadrupling its revenue. In 2012 it overtook Hasbro to become the world's second-largest toy-maker. The number-one toymaker, Mattel, has bought the Canadian maker of Mega Bloks toy bricks in order to fend off the challenge from Lego. It's a remarkable journey by a brand from Billund in rural Denmark, a town so small that the company had to provide it with a hotel.

Adhering to a core value system doesn't mean you limit your options when it comes to product offerings, either. Lego has different options for different levels; it has cross-branded options, options for younger kids, options for older kids, options for adults. It encourages consumers to compete in building events; my brother-in-law (a banker) and my wife's cousin (an engineer and start-up executive) coach a winning Lego team, which they've put together with like-minded friends and their kids. The key here is that all these products and offshoots are aligned in Lego's commitment to creating new ideas and inspiring creativity. It solves one problem and fulfills one need, and it does it in such a way that the value it delivers aligns with its values.

On the other hand, Uber is driving toward failure as it veers from its core proposition. Don't get me wrong; it had a wonderful and insightful idea that disrupted the market with an easy, efficient, and up-to-date way to get transportation anywhere at any time. But before putting in the work to really establish and deliver on that promise consistently, and working all the kinks out, Uber has started to branch out in other directions. It's doing Uber delivery, making dinner reservations, delivering laundry, and delivering ice cream.

Are these activities aligned with its core promise? Not at all. And not only that, but the distractions caused by these offshoots are interfering with Uber's ability to deliver on its core promise consistently. Over the past three months, my Uber experience has failed to deliver. The values that it espoused when it promised to get me from Point A to B at a fair price are worth nothing to me when the company can't deliver. Instead of making me happy, Uber has consistently made me crabby.

When companies get distracted by new propositions and new promises, they act far too hastily, and distraction begets more distraction. Like McDonald's and its bloated menu, or Sears and its trysts with misaligned prospects, they allow themselves to fall into a cycle of malignant growth. But when companies identify the customer problems that they can solve, promise to solve them, and then keep that promise, they provide a value proposition, and they're able to survive in today's Insight Economy. And if their values align with the values of their customers, then they begin to thrive.

Not very complicated, is it?

CHAPTER 10

Give Consumers *Real* Reasons
to Buy Your Products

IN THE INSIGHT ECONOMY, it's not enough anymore to bring products to market just because you *can*. True, the democratization of technology today makes it easy and, therefore, very tempting. Companies born and bred in the Attention and/or Information Economies are organized to think this way. And why not? That is how these companies have grown and scaled over the past several decades. New products tend to drive new trials. They also attract new prospects into the franchise. This allows marketers and companies to show the impact of their actions. Increased revenue is a good metric for the CEO, for the board, and most important, for the analysts. It helps drive increased share price. So why isn't it the best thing for companies to do?

It is. But what companies need to do today is not think of new products *as* new products. Let me illustrate this with a specific example. United Parcel Service (UPS) was founded in 1907 by an enterprising nineteen-year-old, James (Jim) E. Casey, who borrowed $100 from a friend and established the American Messenger Company in Seattle, Washington. Since that time, UPS has become the world's largest package-delivery company and a leading global provider of specialized transportation and logistics services. Delivering millions of packages around the globe is what it does best. A couple of years ago, UPS realized that it needed to evolve some of its services to better serve its small- and medium-sized business customers. These customers were quite mobile, and being stuck at one location awaiting delivery of a package was not the best use of their limited available time. UPS launched a program called UPS My Choice™. UPS My Choice™ gave customers a new level of flexibility and control over home deliveries, with alerts before the first delivery attempt and the power to redirect or reschedule packages to fit their needs. In the couple of years since the inception of this new "product," more than 11 million of their customers have signed up. Although UPS doesn't provide specific information about the program's financial impact in its analyst reports or filings, anecdotal reports say that this may be one of the most successful programs in the company's history. This is because it followed the new model that is required for success in the Insight Economy.

The old model was big new-product launches or big advertising campaigns supporting line extensions. This process took months or years to bring to market. It was capital intensive and time intensive. Today's model is built for speed, effectiveness, and efficiency.

Here's a guideline I mentioned earlier: Launch only a new product or service that costs one-tenth of what it would cost to develop a full product. Figure out a way to evolve it constantly so that it keeps delivering more and more value. Make it able to provide over a hundred times the impact. If the product or service fails, you can quickly reboot and refine it based on what you have learned from your failures. If it succeeds, you continue to evolve it as you chase bigger and better results.

This is what UPS did. When it first launched the My Choice program, it was to manage deliveries around customers' schedules. Today, it continues to evolve My Choice to provide better services as it learns from its customers. UPS now has a premium option for a $40 annual subscription fee. Premium members can reschedule deliveries, have their packages delivered to another address, and schedule deliveries during confirmed time windows, all at no additional cost.

This UPS example is good because it isn't a new-world company; it's a 108-year-old company that survived the Attention Economy, succeeded in the Information Economy, and is actually thriving in the early stages of the Insight Economy by focusing on its customers, using the new model for impact, and earning customers' trust and loyalty with this approach. Customers today demand substance and authenticity. They expect an alignment in true values with the companies they do business with. By creating new products and services that solve their *real* problems in a compelling way, brands become valuable and marketers become growth leaders.

HOW DID WE GET HERE?

As with many of the issues that we've explored in this volume, there are still companies that came of age in the Attention Economy that seem to follow those rules even though most of them no longer apply. I get it. It's very similar with my golf swing. All the habits I picked up when I began playing by myself six years ago reappear magically every time I'm playing under pressure. The same thing happens to marketers, except that they're under pressure all the time. The skills they learned and the rules that worked are the ones they use. It's tempting to stick to the playbook that worked for many years when you don't have a new one for the emerging ecosystem.

But the world of the Attention Economy is light years removed from the world we're living in now. That era was built around a preponderance of new-product launches, the introduction of new brands and new technologies aimed at the large, homogenous American middle class. To stand out in rapidly crowding categories, companies scrambled to innovate. Every few months, a "new and improved" product hit the shelves, often only incrementally different from the previous iteration. And many of these incremental "innovations" weren't really developed for the consumer; they were designed with the financial needs of the company in mind.

For instance, Crest might come out with a toothpaste tube with a flip-top cap. If you were to examine it closely, you might notice that the new cap is easier to use, and the mouth of the opening is slightly wider, meaning that more toothpaste comes out. While you might think, at first glance, *this makes for easier brushing*, really what it's doing is causing you to use more Crest, meaning you'll run out quicker, meaning you're going to have to buy more often. "New and improved" in some cases was code for "planned obsolescence"! The same so-called innovations could be seen with packaging that kept shrinking in increments too small to garner too much attention. As those packages shrank, profit margins grew.

It was an innovation of a sort, but not one aimed at the consumer. In fact, it seemed as time went on that the world was being built around innovation in pricing, packaging, and promotions strategies rather than in products themselves. Because the world at the time was focused on a rather homogenous group of people, this tactic didn't seem to have any drawbacks. When focused on the lowest common denominator—grabbing the attention of a specific group of shoppers—it seemed that any company with enough market share had the ability to do well.

Guess what happened as we moved into the Information Economy? Suddenly, with more segmented and specific information at our fingertips, we were able to see different opportunities for innovation. It was as though additional rungs on the crowded consumer ladder were appearing, and if a brand could produce a product that spoke to a specific segment, that brand could latch onto that rung. So in the toothpaste world, as we mentioned in the last chapter, there were innovations for specific purposes. You could buy Crest for whitening. You could buy Crest for sensitivity. You could have Crest mouthwash, and a Crest toothbrush to boot. Brands were expanding their franchises, under the premise that *more* is the key to *more growth.*

There were brands that made it through this time successfully. Gillette, for example, released new-and-improved razors with more blades, powered with batteries, with Flexball™ technology, and other capabilities to find new and better ways for its customers, both men and women, to get closer shaves with less irritation. All these improvements were designed to solve real customer problems. The same could be said of Crest, which has continued to launch new products to provide comprehensive solutions to help improve the oral health of its customers across all segments. Gillette and Crest are attempting to build Brand Rituals™, creating bonded relationships with their customers. This is the reason they continue to do well. As brands continue to innovate in ways that solve real problems for their customers, these customers not only make the cash register ring, but also recommend the brand to their friends and followers across their social networks. "Hallelujah. This brand really understands me. I never told them what I wanted, I never asked them for what I needed, but they gave it to me anyway."

But not everyone has managed to navigate the shifting world of the Information Economy successfully. The *unsuccessful* brands, such as Circuit City, failed to grasp the context of the real problems they were tasked to solve. Because they failed at this, their businesses failed. Brands that were successful in both eras understood that they serve *real people* who have real problems that need to be solved. The brands that do this well are the brands that survive.

THE INTEL ISSUE

You might be surprised to hear me talk about Intel as an example of how *not* to do things, but there's no escaping the fact that even the biggest and most successful companies make mistakes. Intel Corporation is the largest semiconductor manufacturer in the world today. Intel has changed the world dramatically since it was founded in 1968; the company invented the microprocessor, the "computer on a chip" that made possible the first handheld calculators and personal computers.

By the early 21st century, Intel's microprocessors were found in more than 80 percent of PCs worldwide. This dominance is what caused the problem for Intel. It's not surprising when companies become very successful that they end up focusing on protecting and defending their trees rather than responding to the contextual evolutions in the forest.

In 1996, on revenues of $20 billion, Intel's net income exceeded $5 billion. Four years later, in 2000, it had grown its revenue to $34 billion. Its growth slowed after that; in the following ten years Intel added only $10 billion to its topline.

There are a couple of reasons for these challenges. One, Intel became maniacal in its focus on delivering faster and faster chips for computers, perpetuating Moore's Law. This law is based on an observation made in 1965 by Gordon Moore, co-founder of Intel, that the number of transistors per square inch on integrated circuits had doubled every year since the integrated circuit was invented. Moore predicted that this trend would continue for the foreseeable future. This focus made Intel a bit myopic, causing it to miss the transition from computers to mobile phones and mobile devices.

The second reason for Intel's difficulties is its intent. Its mission statement reads, "Delight our customers, employees, and shareholders by relentlessly delivering the platform and technology advancements that become essential to the way we work and live." This is too broad and too mushy. Nowhere does it indicate that the one thing Intel does well is make chips for technology devices. As we discussed earlier in the book, focus on their deliverables is critical for brands to succeed, especially in the Insight Economy. Intel does become a bit more specific in the objectives it provides its employees, declaring that it wants to extend its silicon technology and manufacturing leadership and deliver unrivaled microprocessors and platforms.

Intel missed its window of opportunity to enter the mobile chip race and has struggled to remain credible for the past decade. In a letter to shareholders in 2012, then-CEO Paul Otellini tried to put a spin on Intel's "mobile edge." At the time, Intel chips were installed in six different smartphones, which included the Lenovo K900 and Safaricom Yolo. Has anyone heard of these phones? I haven't.

Without too many other options, Intel was forced to place a losing bet on the Windows phones because Qualcomm's Snapdragon™ chip has become the primary engine driving Android devices. As we know, spins don't work, so less than a year later, Brian Krzanich replaced Paul Otellini as Intel CEO. The speculation at that time was that Otellini had been shown the door due to Intel's missteps in the mobile market when he was at the helm.

Ironically, Moore's Law is largely behind the shift away from desktop and toward mobile. In June 2014, comScore, a digital research firm, published a report showing that a large cross-section of the mobile market is lost to Intel. The report, titled "April 2014 U.S. Smartphone Subscriber Market Share," actually published the averages of data taken from the first calendar quarter of 2014. What this report showed was the dominance of the Android—iOS duopoly in the mobile market. Taken together, Google and Apple had 93.9 percent of the U.S. smartphone-subscriber market. Microsoft and BlackBerry are at the bottom, desperately trying to stay alive.

A July 8, 2015 article in *Business Insider* asserted, "Windows Phone is all but dead."[17]

On Wednesday (July 8), Microsoft gutted what was left of its handset business by announcing it will cut another 7,800 jobs in the division and take a $7.6 billion write-down on its 2013 acquisition of Nokia.

In an open letter to employees, CEO Satya Nadella said Microsoft will no longer focus on building a "standalone phone business." Instead, it will concentrate its resources on supporting the Windows software that powers Windows Phones and release limited flagship models.

And this is happening at a time when the personal-computer industry is slogging through a decline. It is no wonder that Intel Corp.'s mobile division reported an operating loss of $4.21 billion for 2014, an amount that would erase profits at all but two of the thirty companies on the Philadelphia Stock Exchange Semiconductor Index. They racked up these losses in a business that reported negative sales in the fourth quarter of 2014. Rather than generate revenue, Intel has been paying customers to use its chips in tablets, trying to build a market presence while it brings out new models that they'll want to buy.

Wow. Paying customers to use your product. I hope this bet pays off! Most companies can't afford to lose a fraction of this amount, and they have to ensure that their customers pay to buy and use their products. It is time to pay attention to the principles of the Insight Economy.

[17] http://www.businessinsider.com/even-microsoft-is-giving-up-on-windows-phones-2015-7

Instead of looking to make the next best product, if Intel had looked at the business with an empathetic view of the customer, it would have realized how quickly I was transitioning to devices that freed me from any encumbrances, and it would have leapt to serve me in the way it knows how: With the fastest and most efficient processors in the world. I do hope Intel can turn the corner.

Intel might disagree with my interpretation; it's possible that it might claim it was doing nothing but sticking with its core, something that I advocate heartily throughout this book. But there's an important distinction between sticking to your core and ignoring the world around you. Intel was no longer thinking about solving problems for the customer: It was just focused on solving the problem of how to make its chips faster. Had it carried out its duties to *the customer*, it would have been able to see very clearly that the customer's needs were changing as more customers adopted mobile devices. By losing the ability to see where else the customer might have real problems and real needs, Intel lost the ability to stay ahead of the pack and innovate in the right places.

It's in complete contrast to Eggo, my ritualized breakfast food, which continues to innovate successfully to provide me with better and more varied choices of pancakes, waffles, and breakfast sandwiches so that I can have a good, quick breakfast before running off to my day. This is why the Kellogg Company continues to deliver solid results year-in and year-out.

THE AMAZON ADVANTAGE

I believe I was a bit of a stick in the mud about Amazon earlier in the book. Despite being one of its best and happiest customers, I have described the fractures I have begun to see in the experience, primarily because it has already set the bar so high that any slippage feels like a long fall. Having said this, Amazon is doing a lot of other things *right*. I'd like to tip my hat to Jeff Bezos and his team for innovating and experimenting to continue making the shopping experience better while expanding the scope for the brand.

From the very beginning, Amazon has been ahead of the curve when it comes to fulfilling needs and minimizing the annoyances that characterize the shopping process. The first innovation is obvious— it created an online marketplace for just about anything, whereas before, you'd have to drag yourself out of your pajamas and out to the store. From there, it made a big push for speed. When Amazon first started out, shipping was spotty; you weren't sure when things were going to come to your doorstep. Something bought in the name of convenience might take a week to show up, which was anything but convenient! Fast-forward to now, and you not only have a very quick delivery window, but you've got an option to pay slightly more for guaranteed same-day or next-day shipping. Amazon has continued to streamline its operations in order to fix this pain point. Its ability to communicate throughout the entire process is another thing other brands can learn.

Amazon didn't stop there. Just because it improved something once doesn't mean it doesn't try to improve it again. The company realized that its best customers, like me, would prefer not to pay shipping charges every time we ordered merchandise, considering that we order so frequently. I seem to order something or other literally every day, and sometimes multiple times a day.

Unlike United, who took my custom with it for granted because it gave me points, Amazon decided that the key to a continued relationship with me was an equitable value exchange. I talked about this in Chapter Six as a new model in which brands build relationships with their customers in a reciprocal manner, based on Trust, Respect, and Loyalty. It introduced Amazon Prime: I agreed to pay $79 per year (now increased to $99), for which originally I got free two-day shipping. As any Prime customer who buys frequently from the e-tailer can attest, it doesn't take long for that membership to pay for itself. Well, guess what? Since then, Amazon has continued to make the Prime membership more valuable, adding Prime Instant Video, Prime Music, Prime Photos, Prime Pantry, Amazon Elements, Prime Early Access, Kindle Owners' Lending Library, Kindle First, and Membership Sharing. For an additional $20, I get all these services, some of which I haven't even used yet. It's a bargain! Because a lot of these services address real problems I encounter in acquiring products or content, they are relevant innovations that valuable Amazon customers like me appreciate.

I wish I could say the same thing about Uber. Uber is an example of a company that is emerging in the Insight Economy, but operating in the Information Economy mindset. It seems to be launching new product after new product before it has absolutely refined its original business and operating model. I was a huge fan. I was one of the first adopters and an evangelist for Uber. And for good reason. For people who live in the Chicagoland area, where you have inclement weather at least six months of the year, Uber was the best innovation ever. Being able to get a cab or a black car quickly and effortlessly made my commute much less painful.

That didn't last, however. As the company has begun to focus on trying all sorts of new services, like delivering ice cream, its ability to solve the original problem for me—getting me transportation quickly and effortlessly—has suffered. Over the past few months, I've had numerous instances in which I couldn't get a car from Uber, and the couple of times that I was able to get an Uber "Black Car," I ended up having to pay three to four times the rate (we all know about their infamous fare multiplier, right?). Imagine paying $50+ for a ride from the train station to my office, which normally costs $9 in a cab, including a $2 tip. I was once one of Uber's biggest fans, but now I'm pretty solidly on the record as saying it's doomed if it can't get its head straight and its act together.

There are those who will call me a contrarian for saying what I just did—pointing out that Uber is a smart company that knows what it's doing: Quick delivery for food, quick dry cleaning services, and such also happen to be unmet needs. My point, however, is that unless a new brand first delivers on its core value proposition and does it in a way that's unassailable—that is, unless it consistently and sustainably fulfills expectations—it will lose. In Uber's case, it needs to ensure that its transportation promise is delivered in a way that it becomes a Brand Ritual.

TRANSPARENCY TODAY

Another crucial concept for successful brands in the Insight Economy is transparency. It's a bit of a chicken-or-the-egg issue: If you're not inclined to be transparent, you probably aren't going to be truly committed to your customers, and without transparency from you, your customers won't trust your intentions. Recently, I had an experience with BNSF Metra, a rail transit brand in the Chicago area, that illustrates this point perfectly.

I had a meeting at 9:00 a.m. in the city, so I wanted to try to get to the office early to have some time to settle in and prepare before I had to sit down with my clients. I was at the Metra station at 7:00 a.m. on the dot, planning to take the 7:06 a.m. train. Well past the time that I should have been boarding my train, there was an announcement concerning an incident farther up the tracks that was causing the trains to run late. Ostensibly in an effort to quell any concerns, there was a follow-up announcement that claimed Metra was sorry for any inconvenience and that trains were expected to run between ten and ninety minutes behind schedule.

At that point, I wasn't just irritated that my best-laid plans had been disrupted by a circumstance that, admittedly, Metra couldn't have anticipated. What was really irking me was the absurdly unspecific window of time that Metra was giving me for when I might expect a train. After half an hour, I hadn't seen a single train go by, but I had heard multiple announcements reiterating the window and the "average" of that window, which Metra was estimating to be twenty minutes.

As I stood there trying to figure out my next steps, I couldn't help but wonder why Metra wouldn't just own up to the unpleasant reality: There was a problem and it was taking time to fix it. It could have announced that due to this technical issue, trains would be delayed significantly (the actual delays did last for over two hours) and that commuters should consider making alternate arrangements. Such openness and honesty would have been highly appreciated by almost all the affected commuters, especially me. It would have shown its customers an unexpected side of Metra that would have enhanced their feelings for the company. What *did* it cost Metra to keep spinning the possible wait times? A *great deal* of goodwill.

In today's world, you can't keep anything hidden. If you try, you'll only succeed in irritating your customers, who have an enormous amount of information at their fingertips no matter where in the world they are. There's no time to be bought; information is available instantaneously, and it's nearly impossible to cover up the cover-ups. I remember once, when in line for a flight on United, I saw the pilot actually come out of the jetway to whisper to a gate agent, after which there was a vague announcement about a flight delay. The fact that I had seen this exchange between the pilot and the gate agent definitely didn't help United's case at all, but the bigger issue was that the company was clearly showing lack of empathy for its customers. Instead of treating us like real people with real concerns, it was clearly engaged in some kind of perverse magical thinking: If it didn't tell us what the problem was, the problem would somehow be less of an issue for us.

The reality of the situation was quite different, as it so often is in these cases. For my fellow passengers and me, not knowing what was wrong with the plane did not make the situation better. It didn't make us less irritated. It didn't make our appointments on the other end of our flight magically realign to an acceptable time. It didn't change the truth. It actually did the exact opposite. It made us more frustrated and corroded our relationship with United.

So my charge to brands is simple: *Just tell us the truth!* There's no fooling people these days, of course, but it's more than that. You shouldn't *want* to fool us. You should *want* to solve our real problems, and treat us like we're real people. You should want to do it with integrity, authenticity, and empathy. When you exhibit those qualities, you've got the formula to succeed in the Insight Economy: You understand the real needs, desires, and expectations of your customers. As a brand, when you have that kind of empathy, you're able to solve your customers' problems better than any competitor. This translates to real dollars, real market share, real goodwill—and real success!

CHAPTER 11

The Real Question: Are You Thinking About the Future of Your Business?

FINALLY. We're at the last chapter. I hope you enjoyed reading this as much as I enjoyed writing it. Bringing my narrative to a close is my favorite part. As we discussed in the first chapter, most marketers are so swamped by the data deluge and the hyper-complexity in today's hyper-fast environment that it is hard for them to stay on top of things today, let alone worry about the future.

We don't have a choice. If we decide to act today on any initiative, we will be in the market with it, if we scramble, about six months later. And that's aggressive. To ensure that we're getting to the future first, we have to be thinking constantly about the future of our businesses. Unfortunately, a majority of marketers aren't. Not because they're short-sighted or they don't care about the changes likely to happen. It's just an issue of focus and available time.

Face it: It's harder than ever to be a CMO. Never before have there been so many new technologies and capabilities to keep up with. Never before have there been so many entities, both inside and out of your businesses, demanding your time and attention. It's impossible to think about the future when you're bogged down in the craziness of NOW, trying to keep up with everything going on in this moment. Who has time to think about tomorrow when today seems like it's already out of control?

I completely sympathize with your predicament. I've been there. But I do believe that it's absolutely vital that you continue to think about the future of your business, even if you don't have the time, as this will help make today's programs foundational to tomorrow's outcomes.

To be honest, there was a point a few years ago when I stopped doing this myself. The pace of change had become so frenetic, and there were so many new things to learn, that I gave in to "new-stuff intimidation." I decided that there wasn't any point in thinking about a future in which things would be so different that it was a waste of time to develop plans. I pooh-poohed the idea of strategic planning—the three-, five-, and ten-year strategic plans that we would spend months on during the Attention Economy. I simply didn't think that it was reasonable to think we could even hazard a guess about what the future would look like in that amount of time, let alone develop plans that made sense. With all the talk about living in a hyper-speed, hyper-complex, and hyper-changing environment, I thought it was a waste of time to plan for the future.

I was wrong. We need to plan for the future. How we plan is different. We don't plan details. We don't plan tactics. We don't plan programs. But we do plan where we want the business to be and the kinds of relationships we need to develop and maintain with our most important customers. If you define your destination and focus and prioritize your actions using one singular prism—your core customer—you'll be able to have a better hold on today, tomorrow, and the future.

If your head is swimming with a ton of ideas from this book (not counting your daily to-do list, which is a thousand items long), let's take a step back and simplify things a little bit. I want you to focus on four simple steps to help map the future of your business. Like any regimented routine, when repeated over time, these steps can be a touchstone to return to, a guide for when you're time-starved and data-deluged. These steps can be the way forward, and I hope that when you've had a chance to look them over, you'll join the focused few instead of the harried many out there.

Step 1: Begin with your most valuable customers.

No matter what the future holds, for your brand or for the market, if you understand who your core customers are and what those core customers need, and understand it deeply and personally, you'll always be valued and relevant. Your core customers have aspirations, hopes, dreams, fears, and concerns. They always will. Let these people be your North Star as you navigate into the future. Don't reach for prospects unless they're your customers' twins, and certainly put your core customers first when you look at new markets and opportunities for growth. Begin every discussion with them in mind, and make sure that anything you do is done to make them more bonded with your brand. By doing this, you'll be building a stronger, more profitable, and more sustainable business.

Step 2: Be consistent, and consistently authentic.

Life is unpredictable. An obsession with change and trends is only going to contribute to a sense of unease among your customers. If you aren't steady, if you don't act like an anchor for them, how can they place their trust in you? Don't give these people another thing to be insecure about; the world is already frightening enough. These men and women are living in a world that engenders a consistent sense of angst, insecurity, and fear. The paradigm of prosperity that some of our ancestors grew up in doesn't exist anymore. We're living in a society of scarcity. I'm neither foolish enough nor arrogant enough to assume that anything we can do as marketers will change that, but I am optimistic enough to think that if we can relate to our customers on that basic human level, they'll be more appreciative than not. That is why I am evangelizing the TRL model. As discussed earlier, this stands for Trust, Respect, and Loyalty. Your customers will come to trust you if you consistently deliver on your promise to meet their needs in every interaction. You will earn their respect if your values are consistent with theirs. If you do these things well, over time, you will earn their loyalty by being authentic and by being you.

Step 3: Think globally, act globally. Even if you're not global.

As the world continues to evolve, we move ever closer to fulfilling Marshall McLuhan's prediction that we will become "one village," all bridged together and entwined over space and time through technology. The best brands are going to understand the importance of this global influence, and are positioned to react to it. Successful marketers will need to have a broader, more diverse perspective, and a deeper well of empathy for our fellow people to continue to be relevant in this space, which is somehow expanding and contracting all at once. When you think about the future, you *must* be sure to make room in your mind and practices for a vision of a global future. Because that's not just something that's coming—it's already here, and that global future is here to stay. This is why you need to operate with speed, effectiveness, and efficiency. Create innovations that are one-tenth the cost but that can deliver ten times the value, so that you can accrue a hundred times the impact. This is only possible if you take a global view.

Step 4: Remember: It's about humans.

Despite all the light-speed changes and evolutions we're witnessing, there are some things that I can promise you will stay the same:

- We're human beings. We've been human beings and we're going to *stay* human beings.
- We're not deciles. We're not bits and bytes. We're not big clouds of data.
- We're not stupid, silly, or foolish. Our desires and fears are not dismissible.
- Our hopes and aspirations are what provide you growth.

At the end of it all, underneath all this change, we're very high maintenance. We're very demanding. But we can be extremely loyal.

As we market for tomorrow, we will have much to deal with that will be different; that's a given. But the one constant, the one thing that won't change, is the fact that our customer will be my wife! The lovable, adorable, frustrating, demanding, tough, sometimes hard-to-please but unbelievably loyal customer. She will continue to demand the best from us. Her life, and therefore ours, will get more complicated, but it's still going to be life. We're still going to be living it. So let's team up with her and enjoy it. I've done it for over twenty-six years and I'm lovin' it! So can you.

. . .

Ready to take on the future? I think you are. I know I am. If you're as excited about marketing for tomorrow as I am, please visit **zain.raj.com**. Let's get started.

Continued About the Author Bio

An evangelist for innovation and a strong believer in empowering others, Zain Raj has contributed his insights to The Wall Street Journal, Business Week, Fast Company, Forbes, Crain's, and publications of the nation's top business schools.

Zain's first book *Brand Rituals*™*: How Successful Brands Bond with Customers for Life* was an Amazon marketing and sales best-seller in 2012 and can be found on Amazon.

Zain is a sought-after speaker on the changing marketing land-scape. If you would like to book an event with Zain, or reach out to him, you can contact him at zain@shapiroraj.com.

CPSIA information can be obtained
at www.ICGtesting.com
Printed in the USA
LVOW01*1922031115

460997LV00001B/1/P